Study Skills:
Research-Based Teaching Strategies

A Landmark School Teaching Guide

Patricia W. Newhall

Landmark School, Inc.

Prides Crossing, MA

© 2008 Landmark School, Inc.

Published by Landmark School, Inc.
P.O. Box 227
Prides Crossing, MA 01965

ISBN 0-9713297-2-9

Printed in the United States of America

Contents

Landmark School, Inc.

Preface

Access to high-quality subject matter and challenging content in the classroom is not enough to empower students to become competent learners. If education is to be effective, both teachers and students must have the skills to perform their jobs well. Skilled teachers know their students' educational goals, have a clear sense of the skills students need to meet those goals, and have a repertoire of teaching strategies for empowering students to succeed.

Students, too, must have a clear understanding of their goals and needs, as well as a repertoire of learning strategies to help them process, remember, and express ideas about the material they are exposed to in school. To develop this repertoire, students need to learn and practice strategies that enable them to achieve specific, defined goals.

Students with learning disabilities often fail to develop effective learning strategies independently because of interferences with the way they process information. Whether these students succeed in school depends to a great extent upon teachers' ability and willingness to scaffold their input and students' output of information and ideas.

Study Skills: Research-Based Teaching Strategies identifies many valuable teaching strategies educators can use to help students begin to develop strong learning and study skills. The strategies provide organizational scaffolding that empowers students with learning disabilities to be more successful in school. Explicit instruction and guided practice in managing materials, time, and information and ideas enable students to establish effective habits that can increase their sense of self-efficacy, improve their self-regulation, and enhance their academic performance. Intended as a starting point for teaching study skills, these strategies are a compilation of basic study skills taught at Landmark School from the elementary grades through high school.

Although written to address the particular challenges of educators who work with students with learning disabilities, this guide is useful for all teachers who want to foster students' abilities to learn independently. All students need study skills. When teachers commit to building skills-based instruction into their classes, all students reap the benefits.

Landmark School is dedicated to sharing practical and effective teaching strategies with educators who have limited time to wade through scholarly

Landmark School, Inc.

journals or spend the many hours it takes to translate research findings into effective daily practice. Landmark has been educating students with dyslexia and language-based learning disabilities and differences since 1971. This teaching guide reflects the sum of more than 35 years of accumulated classroom wisdom guided by research and refined through daily classroom practice.

An annotated selected bibliography is included at the end of this book for educators who choose to examine more closely the work of professional researchers from various disciplines.

Acknowledgments

I would like to thank the faculty and students of Landmark School. Students come to Landmark to become successful independent learners. Teachers work at Landmark because they are deeply dedicated to developing the skills of students with learning disabilities. These complementary goals engender dynamic classroom interactions as students and teachers work together to figure out the best approach to any given challenge.

Study Skills: Research-Based Teaching Strategies exists because teachers at Landmark's Elementary/Middle School and High School are so willing to share with their colleagues the strategies and materials that succeed in their classrooms. The Study Skills Department at Landmark High School, headed by Brigitta Allen and Diane Vener, deserves special recognition for its ongoing participation in the Landmark School Outreach Program. Outreach's publications, professional development programs, and online seminars support educators as they help students develop and use study skills across the curriculum.

I would also like to acknowledge the teachers who have participated in the scores of professional development programs Landmark Outreach has facilitated over the years. Each time I lead a workshop or seminar, I learn from the teachers attending and my own teaching approach is enhanced.

Thank you to Joan Sedita and Diane Vener, whose Landmark School publications provided useful exercises and examples for chapter 5. To those who generously offered to read and comment on this manuscript, thank you all: Colleen Kelleher, Suzanne Crossman, Brigitta Allen, and Diane Vener from Landmark; Brother Timothy Paul and Charles L. Newhall from St. John's Preparatory School; Ann Dolbear from the Carroll School; and Carol McInaney from Marblehead Community Charter School.

Finally, I would like to thank Dan Ahearn for his flexibility and his confidence in me, Kathryn Frye for her patience and willingness to listen, Liz Sweibel for her editorial prowess, and the Landmark School Outreach Program's Publications Committee for its unflappable belief in the value of Landmark School teaching guides.

About the Author

Patricia W. Newhall is the Associate Director of the Landmark School Outreach Program. A teacher of literature and writing since 1987, she joined the Landmark School faculty in 1993. She frequently leads workshops for fellow professionals and has written and edited several publications for the Outreach Program. She holds a Master of Arts degree in English from Boston College, and a Master of Science degree in Special Education from Simmons College.

About the Landmark School Outreach Program

Established in 1977, the Landmark School Outreach Program offers a comprehensive professional development program and publications that are based on applied educational research, Landmark's "Six Teaching Principles" and more than 35 years of innovative instruction of students at Landmark School.

Professional Development opportunities include an annual leave Professional Development Institute held during the summer at Landmark School, consulting and on-site programs in schools and districts, and online seminars through LOOP, the Landmark Outreach Online Program. Programs focus on essential topics that support teacher's efforts to help all students learn. Topics include:

- Language-Based Teaching
- Assessment
- Expressive Language
- Reading
- Study Skills
- Writing
- Math

Information about Outreach programs and publications is available online at *www.landmarkoutreach.org*.

About Landmark School

Founded in 1971, Landmark School is recognized internationally as a leader in the field of language-based learning disabilities. A coeducational boarding and day school for elementary, middle, and high school students, Landmark individualizes instruction for each student and emphasizes the development of language and learning skills within a highly structured living and learning environment. Information about Landmark is available online at *www.landmarkschool.org*.

Landmark's Six Teaching Principles

Imagine an instructional hour in which all students are interested and involved. The teacher motivates students by making the material meaningful to them. Information is presented in a variety of interesting ways that engage the range of learning styles in the class. The teacher builds opportunities for success by presenting information in small, sequential steps, and offers positive feedback as soon as students learn and apply a relevant new skill. The teacher provides examples and clear directions for homework, and sets aside a few minutes at the end of class for students to begin the homework assignment. During this time, the teacher answers questions and makes sure each student understands the task. In short, the teacher structures the hour so each student is challenged, works at an appropriate level, and leaves the class feeling successful and confident.

The Landmark School was founded in 1970 to provide this type of structured, success-oriented instruction to students with learning disabilities. Since then, Landmark teachers have continually enhanced and refined teaching strategies to help students learn more effectively. Landmark has shared its teaching strategies with public- and private-school teachers from all over the world through Landmark seminars. All students can and do learn from Landmark's structured, success-oriented instructional models.

At the heart of Landmark's instructional strategies and programs are six teaching principles. They are summarized below.

Teaching Principle #1
Provide Opportunities for Success

Providing students with opportunities for success is key. Failure and poor self-esteem often result when teachers challenge students beyond their ability. Landmark begins teaching students at their current level of ability. This approach improves basic skills and enhances confidence. As Landmark teachers introduce each new skill, they provide basic examples and assignments to build confidence and keep students from becoming overwhelmed. As the information becomes more challenging, teachers assign students easier problems to supplement the more difficult ones. In this way, those students who are having trouble with the material complete at least part of the assignment while they work at understanding and learning to apply new information. Teachers provide students with whatever structure is necessary to help students be successful, such as study guides for tests, templates for writing, and guidelines for projects.

Only with a solid foundation of basic skills and confidence can students make progress. That is why it is key to provide them with opportunities for success.

Teaching Principle #2
Use Multisensory Approaches

Multisensory teaching is effective for all students. In general, it means presenting all information to students via three sensory modalities: visual, auditory, and tactile. Visual presentation techniques include graphic organizers for structuring writing and pictures for reinforcing instruction; auditory presentation techniques include conducting thorough discussions and reading aloud; tactile presentation techniques include manipulating blocks and creating paragraphs about objects students can hold in their hands. Overall, implementing a multisensory approach to teaching is not difficult; in fact, many teachers use such an approach. It is important, however, to be aware of the three sensory modes and to plan to integrate them every day.

Teaching Principle #3
Micro-Unit and Structure Tasks

Effective teaching involves breaking information down into its smallest units and providing clear guidelines for all assignments. This is especially important for students with learning disabilities. Micro-uniting and structuring are elements of directive teaching, which Landmark consistently uses with students. *Micro-uniting* means analyzing the parts of a task or assignment and teaching those parts one step at a time. Teachers organize information so that students can see and follow the steps clearly and sequentially. As students learn to micro-unit for themselves, they become less likely to give up on tasks that appear confusing or overwhelming. Consequently, these strategies enable students to proceed in a step-by-step, success-oriented way.

Teaching Principle #4
Ensure Automatization through Practice and Review

Automatization is the process of learning and assimilating a task or skill so completely that it can be consistently completed with little or no conscious attention. Repetition and review (spiraling) are critical. Sometimes students appear to understand a concept, only to forget it a day, week, or month later. It is not until students have automatized a skill that they can effectively remember and use it as a foundation for new tasks. Teachers must therefore provide ample opportunities for students to repeat and review learned material. For example, the Landmark writing process emphasizes practice and consistency. Students always brainstorm, map/outline, draft, and proofread in the same way. This provides them with an ongoing, consistent review of learned skills.

Teaching Principle #5
Provide Models

Providing models is simple, yet very important. It is one of the most effective teaching techniques. Models are concrete examples of what teachers expect. They do not mean that teachers are doing assignments for students. They are standards to which students can compare their own work. A model or example of a completed assignment serves as a springboard for students to begin the assignment. For example, teachers should give students a model of a sequential paragraph when teaching basic sequential paragraph writing.

Teaching Principle #6
Include Students in the Learning Process

Students are not passive receptacles to fill with information. They come to class with their own frames of reference. Their unique experiences and knowledge affect them as learners and should be taken into account. Therefore, during every exercise, teachers should accept student input as much as possible. They should justify assignments, accept suggestions, solicit ideas, and provide ample time for students to share ideas. Teachers should include students in assessing their own progress by reviewing test results, written reports, and educational plans. Creating and improvising opportunities to involve students in the learning process allows students to become aware of how they learn and why certain skills benefit them. As a result, students are motivated and more likely to apply those skills when working independently. In short, an included student becomes an invested student who is eager to learn.

CHAPTER 1

STUDY SKILLS AND ACADEMIC COMPETENCE

Introduction

Study skills contribute to students' ability to organize, remember, and apply their knowledge. The skills fall into three categories: managing materials, managing time, and managing information and ideas. To gain academic competence, students must learn strategies that make them efficient, effective managers in each of these areas. However, students need more than study skills. They also need literacy skills, proficiency in self-regulation, and a sense of self-efficacy. All of these skills are interconnected and develop interdependently, and are essential for students to become academically competent.

Skills for Academic Competence

Figure 1 shows the three skill areas necessary for academic competence. They develop interactively and dynamically, and are essentially rooted in the interrelated cognitive processes of attention, memory, and executive function. Each skill area is introduced below, followed by a brief explanation of the relationship between executive function and study skills.

Literacy Skills

Though this guide focuses on study skills, a word about literacy must come first, as literacy is the skill set most commonly recognized as essential to academic competence. *Literacy skills* include reading fluency as well as fluency in both oral and written expression. Weak literacy skills put a student at risk academically just as surely as substandard food puts a restaurant at risk of going out of business. Even the most creative chef can only produce a meal as accomplished as the quality and variety of foods he or she has available.

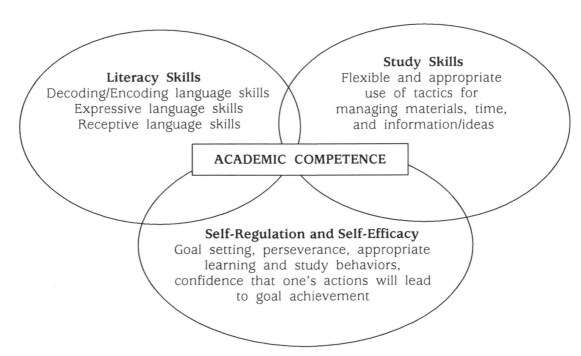

Figure 1. **The three skill areas necessary for academic competence.**

Likewise, students' academic success greatly depends on the depth and breadth of their literacy skills. Attention to literacy skill development must match attention paid to study skill development for students to gain academic competence. (Chapter 5 addresses some basic comprehension skills that are essential for the study skills strategies in chapter 6.) Literacy skills are discussed in more detail in other guides published by Landmark, including the booklet series *Understanding Language-Based Learning Disabilities.*

Study Skills

Study skills include organizational and memory strategies as well as strategies for analyzing tasks, managing time, and integrating new ideas and information. To continue the analogy above, a chef requires more than a variety of high-quality food to produce a fine meal. He or she must also prepare the food in keeping with the restaurant's menu and ensure it arrives at the table on time, at the right temperature, and attractively presented.

If students are to succeed in school, they must develop strong literacy skills *and* strong study skills. To prepare for a test, for example, students must organize materials, choose and use study strategies appropriate to the subject matter, and use their time productively. If they have skills in these areas, they are more likely to demonstrate their knowledge successfully on the test.

Study Skills: Research-Based Teaching Strategies provides essential skill-building strategies for managing materials, time, and information. The strategies are offered as a starting point for students to develop independent study skills.

Self-Regulation and Self-Efficacy

Students must also develop behaviors and attitudes that enable them to put their developing literacy and study skills to appropriate use. Academic competence relies on two related elements that are as critical as literacy and study skills but less observable: self-regulation and self-efficacy. *Self-regulation* is the ability to begin and sustain thinking and behavior that leads to attaining a set goal. Self-regulation includes the ability to manage time, choose appropriate study strategies, evaluate progress toward set goals, and shift to a different plan when progress stalls. *Self-efficacy* is the feeling of confidence that one's actions and behaviors will directly lead to achieving a set goal. Without self-efficacy, students are likely to give up in the face of a challenge and to ascribe any success they have to luck rather than their own skills.

Practicing the strategies in this guide will build students' self-regulation skills and sense of self-efficacy. The strategies work, and when teachers help students see that using them affects their performance on assessments, students begin to understand that their approach to school work positively impacts their grades. Though this seems obvious to adult readers, many students need help evaluating their role in their academic success.

Teachers, parents, and students themselves know that success breeds success. It is essential, then, that students learn the skills they need to succeed in school. Some students develop literacy skills, study skills, and self-regulation and self-efficacy with little guidance. Most, however, require explicit instruction and continuous practice to process the vast array of information they encounter each day efficiently and effectively.

Self-Efficacy

". . . students with higher self-efficacy tend to participate more readily, work harder, pursue challenging goals, spend much effort toward fulfilling identified goals, and persist longer in the face of difficulty . . . students not only need to have the ability and acquire the skills to perform successfully on academic tasks, they also need to develop a strong belief that they are capable of completing tasks successfully" (Hsieh, Sullivan, & Guerra, 2007, p. 457).

Executive Function

Executive function has become a topic of great interest. It describes the brain's skill at accessing and coordinating all its various functions in order to engage in goal-oriented behavior, which is essential to success both in and out of school. Our understanding of the brain has increased tremendously since the advent of functional magnetic resonance imaging (fMRI), which shows the brain at work.

Though researchers have made great strides in understanding how the brain processes language, they do not yet know why some individuals learn more efficiently and effectively than others. Many researchers are focusing on the relationships among the cognitive processes of attention, memory, and executive function on one hand, and school performance on the other. Their studies address difficulties related to intelligence, attention deficit/hyperactivity disorder, social and emotional development, and phonological processing.

While researchers have generated various descriptions of executive function, Brown's (2007) analogy of the brain as a symphony and executive function as its conductor is used here because of its clarity.

> Regardless of their expertise, the musicians need a competent conductor who will select the piece to play, makes sure they start playing at the same time and stay on tempo, fade in the strings and then then bring in the brass, and manage them as they interpret the music. Without an effective conductor, the symphony will not produce good music (p. 23).

Brown also lists six executive functions that work together in various combinations. Effective studying requires effective, efficient coordination of *all* of them.

- *Activation*: organizing, prioritizing, and activating for work
- *Focus*: focusing, sustaining, and shifting attention to tasks
- *Effort*: regulating alertness and sustaining effort and processing speed
- *Emotion*: managing frustration and modulating emotions
- *Memory*: using working memory and accessing recall
- *Action*: monitoring and self-regulating action (p. 24)

The strategies in this guide will not "cure" students with impairments in one or more executive functions. However, together the strategies provide a scaffold that, if masterfully built, supports students' efforts to manage the complex curricular demands placed on them.

The Shift from Teaching Strategies to Teaching Content

In early elementary school, appropriate classroom behavior, a positive attitude, and hard work are all it takes for students to succeed. Teachers commend students who pay attention, follow directions, and exhibit these skills. Teachers know that children of this age need explicit instruction and a great deal of practice to master the strategies that allow them to succeed in school. They take responsibility for ensuring that students acquire skills and develop and practice strategies for managing materials, time, and information. They explicitly teach students to manage schoolwork and homework. A daily schedule on the board lets students know what they've accomplished and what is coming next, a silly poem helps them recall exceptions to spelling rules, a song prompts them on the correct order of arithmetic operations, and a brightly colored folder in their backpack provides a visual reminder of homework.

As students move into upper elementary and middle school, teachers' focus generally shifts from teaching strategies to teaching content. The pressures of state-mandated testing and the need to prepare students for the increased demands of high school drive teachers to introduce an extraordinary amount of information. Strategies are still taught, but often less explicitly and with fewer opportunities for guided practice. Students are expected to gather meaning from what they read and hear, write essays, create projects, complete homework, and prepare for quizzes and tests with increasing independence. Appropriate behavior, a positive attitude, and hard work are recognized in middle school, but it is good grades that mark success from this point on. A good grade assumes masterful literacy skills, study skills, and self-regulation skills.

It's Worth It

Catherine, a Landmark School senior who was researching and writing an essay for a senior project, was required to follow her teacher's system for staying on schedule and keeping track of research. Catherine complained throughout the term about what she felt was "useless extra work" but followed the required system because she wanted to earn an A in the class.

When she finished the project, she wrote to her teacher in her self-evaluation: "I have to admit that I really hated doing this, but you were right. When I went to write my essay, it was really easy because everything was organized, and all my ideas were already connected. It only took me a couple of hours to finish it. I couldn't believe it!! I know it's not perfect, but I worked really hard on it. I was really scared about this project because I've never had to do anything this long. I guess I've learned how I should do my projects at college."

Catherine earned a B+ on her project, and an A in the class. She recently graduated from a four-year college.

While responsibility for acquiring skills and practicing strategies falls increasingly on students as they move through their school career, many students lack strategies for managing academic and extracurricular demands. Even with appropriate behavior, a positive attitude, and hard work, these students find themselves struggling or failing in school.

Study Skills and Language-Based Learning Disability

Language-based learning disability (LBLD) refers to a spectrum of difficulties related to the understanding and use of oral and written language. Individuals with a language-based learning disability are at a profound disadvantage in an academic setting, where most information and idea exchange occurs through the medium of language. Difficulty acquiring fluent language can affect students not only when they read and write, but also when they think and study. Why? Effective learning requires the use of what is sometimes called *internal language*, which is the inner voice we use to guide us through tasks.

Students with a language-based learning disability require specialized, intensive, individualized instruction to gain competence and confidence with language. In addition to literacy skills, these students must also acquire the study skills and self-regulation skills to plan, execute, and evaluate their performance on complex tasks. Many studies have demonstrated that students with learning disabilities do not develop these skills independently. However, when given explicit strategy instruction and continuous practice and monitoring, these students are more likely to succeed in academic tasks (Swanson, 1999).

> ### "Just Study Harder"
>
> "The admonition to study harder in order to succeed academically presents barriers for students with LD who have not developed an effective reading system, do not understand the importance of good notes, do not know how to organize their study time and manage their academic assignments, or do not know how to approach test-taking situations in an effective manner" (Baer, 1997, p. 126).

Meeting the Need

Teaching students to develop their study skills requires *skills-* or *strategy-based instruction*, which differs from traditional content instruction. Its primary goal is to help students develop the skills they need to comprehend and express content.

Strategy-based instruction works like good athletic coaching. Without coaching, for example, few tennis players learn how to grip and rotate their racquets to place returns purposefully. They learn when a coach models the grip, racquet, and body position for a particular type of return, then helps them. The coach hits easy shots for players to practice, offers supportive feedback, then increases the difficulty as players master the skill. A good coach does not show players a new strategy and then expect perfect execution during a match.

In school, however, students are often expected to demonstrate a skill — taking notes, for example — without having had the modeling, coaching, and practice to master it. Students, like athletes and cooks, need to learn a variety of strategies to manage challenges, and teachers need to be their coaches.

Strategy-based instruction is essential for students with a language-based learning disability because most will not develop the skills they need on their own. It carries the important benefit of putting students in control of their learning. The feelings of self-efficacy that researchers highlight as part of academic competence can only begin to develop when students feel they have the skills to rise to a given challenge and find success.

CHAPTER 2

THE "TEACH FIRST™" LESSON PLANNING STRATEGY

The success of the Suzuki method for teaching violin is a compelling example of how accessible difficult material becomes when it is appropriately modeled, explicitly taught, and regularly practiced with guidance. When six-year-olds who are not virtuosos can play the violin in an enjoyable way, we know the teaching methodology is the key.

Too often in school, students are asked to perform before they are ready. Teachers assume that students come to class with the necessary skills to meet expectations for their grade or level. It is only when teachers collect their notebooks, for example, or ask them to sum up the day's lesson at the end of class, that teachers realize how profoundly diverse students' skills actually are. Though a few students usually come to class as fully independent learners who require only compelling content and clear expectations to be successful, most come needing strategy instruction. They have a patchwork of knowledge, experience, and skills, and need teachers who can help them integrate these bits and pieces into a coherent set of abilities.

Setting Realistic Expectations

Reading teachers often point to the shift in expectations that takes place between the third and fifth grades, when students are expected to transition from learning to read to reading to learn. Before that shift, students participate in reading groups that focus on phonics and sight words, as well as on fluent decoding (i.e., the automatic recognition and grouping of words that is the bridge to comprehension). After that shift, students are expected to be independent readers who can decode, comprehend, remember, and express the ideas from an assigned reading.

During and after this transition, many students begin to struggle in school. We often assume that if a child can read (or hear) it, everything else will (and should) fall into place. This is false. Even those students who have learned to decode text fluently may have undeveloped or underdeveloped comprehension, memory, and expressive language strategies.

Reading is not the only area in which teachers expect increased independence. Many schools begin to shift their focus away from skill development — _how_ to learn — and toward content mastery — _what_ to learn — sometime between the third and fifth grades. Students who have not developed solid decoding, comprehension, writing, and study skills by that time are left to cobble together strategies as best they can or seek extra help after school. Or, they are placed in special education.

A conversation with the father of a middle-school child named Karen stands as a clear example. Karen is motivated and generally successful in school, but received poor grades on her most recent report card. According to her teacher, Karen's homework and class notes are weak, and she does poorly on tests because she doesn't get all the information into her notes. Karen's school has an academic support center that teaches the useful and popular Cornell method for taking notes. (Landmark's note-taking strategies are based on this method.) When Karen's father asked if the Cornell method was being taught in class, he was told that it is only taught to those students who have been identified as needing extra support. His daughter is not among those students. From the school's point of view, Karen (and most students) is capable enough that note-taking strategies should not have to be taught and practiced in class. From her father's perspective, Karen is experiencing anxiety about her ability to do well in school and developing a negative attitude about homework.

This example begs the question, _Why doesn't the school teach all students to take notes?_ If it did, many bright and capable students would succeed without being identified as needing extra help. One response is that teachers think they do teach note-taking. They explain what note-taking is and demonstrate it using an example, then expect students to take notes independently. This is a bit like teaching children to tie their shoes by showing them once then expecting them to do it themselves.

Another response is that teachers want to challenge students to develop the skill on their own, in much the same way as parents might throw their child into a lake and yell "Swim!" Some children will actually swim, just as some will actually learn to take notes. Many will panic, however, splashing and kicking their way to the shore and hating every minute of it. Others will give up and sink until someone dives in to save them. Yet almost every child can learn to swim if properly taught, just as almost every child can learn to take notes.

How do we remedy this situation? We cannot change the educational system overnight. We can only offer suggestions and encouragement to engage in the kind of teaching that makes it possible for many more students to develop academic competence without being identified as disabled or in need of extra help.

What the Research Tells Us

While study skills instruction should reflect research-based best practices, the body of research is slim (compared to research on reading, for example). Even so, the research does tell us — and practical experience shows us — that students learn best when teachers carefully plan lessons and units to maximize every opportunity for students to develop and master skills and understand content.

The research further asserts two clear findings. First, explicit instruction (including modeling) and guided practice of study strategies improves academic performance. The gradual release of responsibility model for instruction offers a good foundation (Pearson & Gallagher, 1983). As students demonstrate mastery of a strategy, teachers gradually withdraw guidance. When students begin to generalize the strategy to novel situations, teachers provide further guidance as needed.

Second, effective study skills instruction extends beyond practicing strategies like highlighting and summarizing; students also need to learn and practice self-regulatory skills. As explained in chapter 1, the framework for academic competence includes both self-regulatory and study skills, as well as literacy skills.

Teach FIRST™

Effective lesson planning takes into consideration not only what is to be taught, but how it is to be taught. A wealth of formal research supports each element of the Teach FIRST™ lesson planning strategy, which is summarized in Table 1. The model's acronym conveniently summarizes the essential steps for teaching content and assessing mastery.

Table 1. Teach FIRST™: A Summary	
Teach FIRST Step	**Teaching Strategies**
Facilitate input of new information and ideas	• Present information and ideas directly, sequentially, and in a visually organized way. • Show students how information and ideas relate to what they have already learned and what they will learn next.
Integrate learning strategies and skills	• Explicitly teach, model, and practice learning and study strategies that enable students to demonstrate their knowledge and skills successfully.
Review and practice repeatedly	• Provide many opportunities for students to practice learning and study strategies.
Synthesize and generalize information and ideas	• Build in class time for students to elaborate on and connect ideas and information. • Create opportunities for students to apply newly acquired knowledge and skills to novel situations.
Test for mastery	• Test students on material they have independently and successfully practiced.

Closing Thoughts on Teach FIRST™

The Teach FIRST™ model, an outgrowth of Landmark School's Six Teaching Principles, reflects an ideal that is tremendously challenging to implement given the complexities of diverse, crowded classrooms and the p ressure on teachers to cover content. Teachers should begin with small steps and build toward the ideal. This teaching guide focuses on the second step, which is to *integrate* learning strategies and skills. Other steps are of equal importance, and students benefit from any consistent efforts teachers make to implement them.

CHAPTER 3

MANAGING MATERIALS

Introduction

Think of it: Electricians arrive at a customer's home to do work and ask if they can borrow tools. A lacrosse team runs onto the field for the big game without their helmets or chest pads. Paramedics respond to a 911 call but leave the first-aid kit at the fire station. Unacceptable? Of course. The electricians would go out of business. The lacrosse players would be benched. The paramedics would be suspended. To do their jobs, these people need instant access to specialized equipment and tools. So do students. Yet we often hear: "I forgot my book." "I lost my binder." "I didn't print out my homework." "Can I borrow a pen?"

Students' difficulties with managing their school materials are regularly referred to in teachers' and parents' conversations. Despite reminders and suggestions, some students just cannot seem to get or stay organized.

Students have difficulty for many reasons. As with any effective instruction, the need is to identify the cause of the difficulty, then design teaching to resolve it. The student profiles below illustrate three potential reasons for some students' disorganization — lack of motivation, lack of time, and lack of skill. If these sound familiar, it is because they are the three most often-cited reasons for students' failure to achieve at expected levels.

Student Profiles

Chris

Chris comes to most classes without pens and notebooks. He sometimes comes without books. Jim, a friend of his, always has a pen or paper handy he can borrow. The teacher usually has an extra handout, and another student is always willing to move his or her desk over so Chris can look on at the textbook.

Chris has a reputation for being disorganized, and does not pay much attention to teachers' reminders to bring his materials. His teachers know he has the skills, for he never forgets his lunch and is always prepared for afternoon sports. Chris has little motivation to keep track of his own materials. He gets good grades, and other students do not seem to mind his habit of borrowing. Over time, Chris has developed *learned helplessness* in managing his materials — behavior that reflects a lack of motivation to take responsibility for his actions.

Chris needs teachers to help him take responsibility for managing his materials by making the incentives for doing so irresistible and the consequences for failing to do so significant. A teacher-created materials list linked to grades or rewards and consequences would help Chris begin to take responsibility.

Rosana

Rosana's school has three minutes of passing time between classes. Frequently, teachers distribute handouts and give homework assignments at the end of class. Rosana writes too slowly to take down all the homework details and still make it to her next class on time. By the time Rosana starts her homework at night, she has lost track of her handouts and forgotten the details of the homework. She often wishes she had the time to get organized because she knows how. But even with the motivation and the skill, Rosana lacks the time to manage her materials.

Rosana needs teachers who allow students to hole-punch and file their handouts and write down their homework assignments before the end of class, or who can help her develop a different strategy for getting organized given the time constraints. A color-coded folder system or a manila folder with sections where she can quickly slide handouts would probably help. Rosana might also request the week's homework from her teachers in advance.

Rashid

Rashid's parents call him "a walking cyclone," and his teachers are exasperated by his lack of organizational skills. His bedroom is a disaster, his locker is bursting at the seams, and his binders and notebooks are virtually unusable. He can never find what he needs when he needs it. Rashid takes good notes but never dates them and frequently writes on whatever page to which he opens his notebook. He does his homework, but usually cannot find it to turn in. He misses out on sports because he forgets his shoes or uniform. He jokes about his messiness so people won't know how badly he feels about it. Rashid has the motivation and the time to manage his materials, but he lacks the skills to create and follow a logical system.

Rashid needs teachers who can explicitly teach him basic materials management and who can monitor and guide him as he learns. Teachers willing to provide a short list of goals, explicit instruction, guided practice, and consistent feedback would see Rashid begin to develop the skills he needs.

Chris, Rosana, and Rashid all need help managing their school materials. They need explicit teaching, consistent modeling and practice, and sensible assessment of their skill development.

Teaching Students to Manage Materials

Materials management skills empower students. They help students be productive in school and avoid time-wasters and anxiety-producers like lost homework, forgotten lunch money, and unsigned permission slips. Even though the research on the effectiveness of teaching materials management skills is slim, the work that has been done indicates that these skills are essential for academic and career success.

While an individual teacher or parent may help a student create an organizational system, it needs to meet the requirements of all teachers and classes. Because this can be challenging, one of the most effective ways to teach materials management is for a school, or a team of teachers, to settle on one system for all students. The system should be designed to account for everything students need to participate in the school day and do their homework, including their books, papers, pencils, and equipment. Ongoing visual and oral reminders of the system help students stay on track, as do rewards for consistent use of the system.

The success of an organizational system depends on its usefulness to students. The point of keeping materials organized is to make learning more efficient and effective. If materials are accessible, students can manage time and assimilate information more effectively. Classroom activities should reinforce these connections. For instance, teachers might allow students to refer to their materials during a pop quiz. Students who use the system to stay organized will do well.

Once a system that works for most students is consistently implemented, educators can make changes to suit individual needs, since no single system works for every student. Teachers need to help students create a system that works for them and help them use it consistently.

Goal, Objectives, and Prerequisites

The goal of teaching materials management is to help students develop and follow a routine to manage their school materials.

The learning objectives are for students to be able to:

- create and maintain an organized workspace at home

- create and maintain an organized desk, locker, or backpack

- learn and maintain the master filing system for their papers

- learn and maintain an organizational system for their digital materials

- create and use systems to navigate transitions successfully

To be successful, students must already be able to label papers with their name, the day, and the date; categorize materials according to stated terms (e.g., put all science materials into the red folder); read or hear a list of directions and follow it; and create a word processing document.

Home Workspace

Purpose

There is a lot to be said for the old saw, "A place for everything and everything in its place." An organized work and living space is both calming and motivating. When we have to spend an hour cleaning up just to make space to work, we expend our energy on a different goal.

Students need routines for keeping their living and working spaces clean, neat, and organized. Although teachers cannot control students' home workspaces, they can discuss how a well-organized space contributes to academic success with parents and students. Teachers can also send home suggestions or a checklist for setting up an efficient home workspace. Last, teachers can model effective organizational skills by keeping their own materials and the classroom orderly.

Materials

A well-organized living and workspace should have:

- shelves or crates to store books neatly

- a dresser or cubbies to store clothing neatly

- storage bins, boxes, drawers, or shelves to store toys, equipment, and the like

- a sturdy desk or table with a comfortable chair of the right height

- a good light for reading and working

- a junk bin or drawer for things that do not have a set location (which should be cleaned out weekly)

- a small filing cabinet or box to store study guides for each class

- a bulletin board for posting photos, rewards, reminders, and such

In addition, some families set up a physical mailbox for each child. It serves as a centralized, consistent place for parents to leave children reminders, signed permission slips, motivational notes, and other communications.

Steps

Teachers (and parents) should recognize that most students want a room and workplace that is orderly and accessible, but often lack the skills to envision, create, and maintain it. By following certain steps, families can get the process of establishing order and routine under way.

The first step is for the parent and child to clean up the living space and decide together where things should "live." The key is to make sure the system makes sense. Sometimes the best way to start is to notice where clutter collects. For instance, one ten-year-old would deposit all his papers, pencils, and puzzle books on the easy chair in his room. The mother placed a plastic bin on the floor next to the chair so he could put it all in there instead. The child's physical gesture was the same, just slightly redirected. Nothing was lost, the chair was usable, and the area looked neat and organized. For younger children, parents can label drawers, bins, and shelves.

> ### Organizing a Home Workspace
>
> 1. Clean up the living space and decide where things should "live."
>
> 2. Establish routines for maintaining the workspace.
>
> 3. Reinforce the advantages of keeping an organized living and workspace.

Once the child's living and workspace is orderly, the need is to establish routines for maintaining it. Some guidelines are listed below.

- Take photographs of the organized room and post them so children can make the room match the picture when they are told to clean up.

- Establish a reward schedule for children who maintain the organizational system.

- Encourage children to work at the desk or table for at least part of the homework routine every night.

- Establish a five-minute clean-up routine at a set time every day. For younger children, this can be part of the bedtime routine.

- Create a routine of loading backpacks and gear bags the night before so they are ready to go first thing in the morning.

Mastering the Routine

The key to creating mastery in the child is for teachers and parents to model, model, model. It is one thing to help children get organized and another to model organizational strategies in our own behavior. Both are necessary to a child's success.

On a regular basis, teachers and parents should reinforce the advantages of keeping an organized living and workspace. Positive comments keep children aware of the time they save by managing their materials. A parent might say, "Your room is so neat! Usually it takes an hour to clean it up. Now you can do something fun. How would you like to spend that hour?"

When efforts at managing materials fail, the natural consequences can be educational. If a student loses a library book, he or she may have to pay for it. Similarly, if a child, parent, or pet steps on a project because the student left it on the floor, the student might have to redo it. Although these consequences alone will not cause the student to get organized, they contribute to his or her overall experience of materials management instruction and practice.

As with all routines, the key to success is consistency. Although it is fine to tweak the established organizational system to meet a child's changing needs, it is best to stick to one system until it is thoroughly ingrained.

Backpacks, Desks, and Lockers

Purpose

The purpose of maintaining an organizational system for backpacks, desks, and lockers is for students to have fast, easy access to their learning tools.

Materials

Students need to stock their desks, lockers, and backpacks with an inventory of:

- pens, pencils, highlighters, crayons, and markers

- pencil sharpeners, erasers, and rulers

- calculators, staplers, hole-punchers, and scissors

- digital storage devices, such as USB keys and CDs

- binder clips, paper clips, sticky pads and index cards

- boxes or pencil cases big enough to hold everything and that close securely

Steps

Backpacks

By keeping a toolkit in their backpacks, students are always prepared as they travel between classes and between school and home. The toolkit should have all the basic materials students need. Younger students who have their own desks at school should develop the routine of transferring the kit to their desk in the morning and returning it to their pack in the afternoon. Alternatively, they can have one toolkit that stays in the desk and a duplicate for the backpack. More information on the backpack is provided later in this chapter, when we discuss the master filing system.

Another strategy is to create a materials list with the heading *Things to Remember*. The list can be laminated and attached to the child's backpack with a metal ring. With older students, brainstorming strategies for remembering materials can be effective. For example, one high-school sophomore rejected the laminated list but was happy to write the list on her backpack in indelible fluorescent green marker.

Desks or Lockers

The first step in organizing a desk or locker is to empty the space out. Teachers or parents then help students come up with a logical system for storing materials. For example, textbooks are best stored with their spines visible for easy identification. Workbooks and notebooks might be best kept on the left side of the desk or in a separate space in the locker.

> **Organizing Desks or Lockers**
>
> 1. Empty the desk or locker.
> 2. Devise a logical system for storing materials.
> 3. Post a photograph of the organized space and a list of materials.
> 4. Set ten minutes aside each week to organize the space.

Once the desk and locker are organized, posting a photograph of it nearby gives students a visual cue for keeping the space organized. Posting a list of materials that should always be in the desk or locker is another valuable strategy.

Last, it is wise to set time aside each week for a whirlwind organizational activity. By spending ten minutes throwing out trash, rearranging books, and filing loose papers, students easily and efficiently maintain the system.

Mastering the Routine

Organizing backpacks, desks, and lockers is a sizeable project. To avoid overwhelming students, it is best to start small and work up to the overall system. Teachers and parents should begin with the toolkits, checking to ensure students are keeping them organized and in the right places. The next tasks are to organize backpacks, desks, and lockers.

Most students will not stick to the system unless they are monitored and provided with some external motivation. Rewards, like bonus points for grades or prizes, can be effective. Some teachers allow students to experience the consequences of not maintaining the system. For instance, students who forget their calculators, rulers, or other materials receive an F for daily class participation.

When teachers and parents consistently provide instruction and support and clearly enforce expectations and consequences, most students master the system.

The Master Filing System: Paper

Purpose

The purpose of the *master filing system* is to help students keep all their class-work and homework papers in one place that provides easy, logical access.

Materials

The master filing system requires a master student binder *or* a master student folder *plus* a master student file.

- The *master student binder* is a full-size, sturdy, three-ring binder, preferably with a zipper around the edges. It includes dividers for each class, plastic page protectors, looseleaf paper, and a three-hole punch designed to fit into the three-ring binder.

- An alternative approach is the *master student folder*. For each class, students have one plastic report folder with storage flaps, page protectors, and looseleaf paper. Ideally, each class folder is a different color. To engage students in the organizational process, a good project is for them to purchase or make book covers that match their folders. Students keep a three-hole punch in their desks or backpack toolkits.

- The *master student file* is a sturdy accordian file or a container for hanging files, such as a file cabinet or crate. It should have enough sections or hanging files to hold a full year's school-work and be at least 12 inches deep. This file may be kept at home (a bit risky) or in the classroom.

Steps

Teachers begin by explaining the master filing system to students, and showing them a sample system. Teachers reinforce that the master student binder or folder goes back and forth to school on a daily basis. The binder or folder is required for all schoolwork and homework, from referring to notes or reference information in class to filing completed homework so it is ready to turn in.

Once students have their materials, they label their binder dividers or folders for each class. They place note-taking paper in each binder section or folder as well as a few page protectors for important reference information (e.g., periodic table, multiplication facts, frequently misspelled words, and homework buddy lists).

Setting Up the Master Filing System: Paper

1. Label binder dividers or folders for each class.

2. Place note-taking paper and page protectors in each binder section or folder.

3. Take notes on paper from the appropriate binder section or folder. Note the class and date.

4. File notes and materials correctly.

5. File returned tests or projects..

In class, teachers remind students to take notes on paper from the appropriate binder section or folder. (See note-taking in chapter 6.) Teachers also remind students to write down the class and date for easy filing should papers go astray. Students file handouts, returned quizzes, and the like in the section of the binder or folder that corresponds to the class.

Once teachers schedule a unit test or project, students start a study guide by gathering their notes and handouts (see chapter 6). By the day of the test or project deadline, students should have a complete study guide in the appropriate section of their master student files. When teachers return the unit tests or projects, students attach them to their study guides. This process gives students a comprehensive reference to review for midterms and finals, conveniently stored in their master files. It also empties students' folders, leaving them ready to be refilled with the next unit's papers.

Mastering the Routine

As with any routine, consistent use and guided practice are the keys to success. Students need to develop good habits, including promptly three-hole punching and filing their handouts.

The key is for students to clean out their binders or folders regularly. Ideally, the clean-out becomes part of preparing for a unit test or project. If teachers assign projects that require students to use all of the information from a unit, students begin to see how the system benefits them.

The Master Filing System: Digital Files

Even students who have mastered organization of their paper-based materials may have difficulty keeping track of their digital files. Some students need explicit instruction for how to organize their computer materials logically.

Purpose

The purpose of a master filing system for digital files is for students to keep all their computer work organized for easy, logical access.

Materials

Students who do not carry a laptop computer generally have three choices for organizing their digital files. They can use a student network folder on the school's computer system (which is often inaccessible from home), a USB key, or a CD-RW with a plastic or cardboard case.

Steps

Students' computer files should be organized in the same way as their paper files. They create one folder for each class. Within that folder, they create subfolders to organize home-work, essays, notes, and other class materials.

Students must learn to save their work frequently and to print their work out as a backup. Learning the difference between *Save* and *Save As* helps them know exactly where the computer saves their files. Students should understand that when they click *Save* from an open word processing document, the computer saves the

> ### Setting Up the Master Filing System: Digital Files
>
> 1. Create one digital folder for each class.
> 2. Create appropriate subfolders for class materials.
> 3. Give documents specific names.
> 4. Save work frequently (using Save As).
> 5. Print work out as a backup.

document to the default location. Informed use of *Save As* ensures that they can save their documents in appropriate, easy-to-find folders.

It is essential that students learn to name their documents clearly. For example, naming a document *Essay* is vague, while naming it *American Revolution Essay* is specific.

Mastering the Routine

To manage digital files successfully, students need to develop good habits, including consistently using one word processing program, specifically naming their documents, saving documents in the correct folders, and printing out and filing hard copies of their digital work into their master filing system.

To keep their computer folders tidy, students should regularly delete any materials no longer in use (e.g., early drafts already printed and filed in the paper-based master filing system). Ideally, the digital clean-out occurs along with the clean-out of paper files as students prepare for a unit test or project.

Closing Thoughts on Managing Materials

Transitions are difficult for many students, yet they navigate hundreds every day. During transitions, students' strategies for managing materials often break down — a binder gets left on the desk in the student's bedroom or a backpack is forgotten at the baseball field. Establishing a comfortable organizational routine to follow during transitions goes a long way toward easing the stress and anxiety some students feel.

Teachers and parents should help children develop standard routines for keeping their materials organized during such transitions as:

- getting up in the morning
- getting ready to go to school
- getting to school
- starting the school day
- moving from class to class
- taking breaks (recess, lunch)
- getting ready to go home (or to extracurricular activities)
- getting home from school (or from extracurricular activities)
- starting and finishing homework
- preparing for the next day

 CHAPTER 4

MANAGING TIME

Introduction

Most people find managing their time a challenge. Balancing the requirements of work with family and friends and flexing to accommodate the unexpected are skills that develop over a lifetime. A Web search on time management turns up close to seven million hits, ranging from articles on college Web sites to seminars for professionals to self-help. Many books also offer strategies for time management. In our busy society, time management skills are essential for success. Luckily, we can teach students some basic strategies to help them make more efficient use of their time.

Ironically, teaching time management strategies challenges teachers' time management in the classroom. Teachers are under tremendous pressure to empower students to be successful learners. Students must demonstrate literacy and mathematical skills, as well as mastery of content, on informal and formal assessments throughout their school years. It is difficult for teachers to justify using classroom time to teach students to manage their materials and time.

Practically speaking, though, many students do not develop these skills on their own. Explicit instruction and guided practice are as important to students' success in managing their time as they are to developing literacy and mathematical skills. Although time management skills are not explicitly measured on achievement tests, they contribute a great deal to students' academic competence. For students with language-based learning disabilities (as well as attention deficit/hyperactivity disorder and other disabilities), good time management skills can make the difference between academic success and failure.

Students have difficulty managing time for different reasons. As with any effective instruction, teachers must identify the cause of the student's difficulty, then design teaching to address it. The scenarios below illustrate three potential reasons for students' difficulty: lack of motivation, lack of clear opportunities to complete tasks throughout the day, and lack of time management skills. Not coincidentally, these are the same three reasons most often cited for students' failure to achieve at expected levels. Also, these reasons are not mutually exclusive; a student may be unmotivated because he or she lacks the skills to be successful and has given up.

Student Profiles

Marina

Marina is often late to classes and after-school activities. Her homework is frequently incomplete, and she regularly complains that she did not have enough time to finish. However, Marina has the skills to manage her time. She reminds the teacher when class is over, and she is usually one of the first to get on the lunch line. During in-class reading or writing assignments she is quite focused and productive. When her teachers hold her accountable for timeliness by offering rewards or issuing consequences, Marina arrives to class on time and with her completed homework.

Marina needs teachers who proactively help motivate her to manage her time by creating and consistently implementing a system of rewards and consequences.

David

David arrives where he needs to be on time, but his homework completion is erratic. He always has an excuse for not completing tasks, and points out his many obligations outside of school (violin lessons, varsity sports, babysitting job, etc.). David has the most trouble completing long-term assignments and preparing for tests and exams, but he frequently fails to complete even short worksheet-type assignments. David's reading and writing skills are solid, and his classwork is high in quality.

David needs teachers to help him set priorities and plan how to use his time outside of school.

Charletta

Charletta is late for everything and rarely completes classwork or homework. In class, she frequently "gets stuck" and fails to move on until the teacher notices and either answers her question or encourages her to skip the difficult parts and move on. Her parents report that she spends a great deal of time on her homework, but agree that she does not seem to accomplish it efficiently. Charletta tends to spend time on minor tasks (such as changing fonts and margins on an essay) then runs out of time for major tasks (such as elaborating on her ideas in the essay).

Charletta needs teachers to help her prioritize her obligations, more accurately estimate time requirements for specific tasks, and budget her time wisely.

Marina, David, and Charletta need help developing time management skills in different ways. They need strategies that are explicitly taught, consistently modeled and practiced, and sensibly assessed.

Teaching Time Management

Time management skills facilitate students' ability to set goals and map out plans for fulfilling academic, extracurricular, work, and family responsibilities. These skills develop slowly, and students often fail to recognize their progress. Perhaps one student completes homework earlier than in the past, or another gets an A on a long-term project because it was carefully done in small segments rather than in a last-minute rush. Teachers should routinely make students aware of how they manage their time so they can see how their behavior can directly lead to improved performance.

To help students link time management with classroom success, teachers can give two grades for assignments and projects. One is the performance or achievement grade — that is, the final product grade. The other is the process grade. It evaluates students' skill at using assignment books, task analysis and time estimation, or getting to class and turning in work on time. If school policy allows for it, teachers can give both an effort and a performance grade, with time management skills averaged into the effort grade. An alternative to double-grading is to give certificates or rewards to students who demonstrate time management skills.

One of the most effective ways to teach time management is for a school, or a team of teachers, to settle on one system for all students and use it consistently. The system should be designed to help students manage long- and short-term school tasks as well as their other responsibilities. Spending time on the system in class, issuing ongoing reminders, and giving rewards all help students stay on track.

Goal, Objectives, and Prerequisites

The goal of teaching time management is to help students develop and follow a routine to manage their obligations and free time both in and outside of school.

The learning objectives are for students to be able to:

- use the strategic calendar system

- incorporate task analysis and time estimation into their strategic calendars

- demonstrate flexibility and set informed priorities when they have competing demands on their time

To be successful, students need to know how to read a clock, how many hours are in a day, how many days are in a week, how many weeks are in a month, and so on. Students also need to know how to read a daily, weekly, and monthly calendar. Students should be able to state how many minutes, days, weeks, or months must pass before a scheduled event.

Basic Time Management Skills

Task Analysis and Time Estimation Skills

Being able to tell clock time is different from understanding the concept of time. Many students can read the clock perfectly well, but when asked to estimate how long an assignment will take, they can seldom provide an accurate answer. While some grossly underestimate the time required and set themselves up for disappointment and frustration, others greatly overestimate and feel overwhelmed before they even begin. Developing a sense of their individual task pace is essential for students to learn time management.

To estimate time with any accuracy, students also need to know the steps required to complete a task. *Task analysis* is the process of identifying what needs to get done to finish a given undertaking — whether it is a homework assignment or a long-term project like a research paper. Students sometimes do not recognize that a single homework assignment might

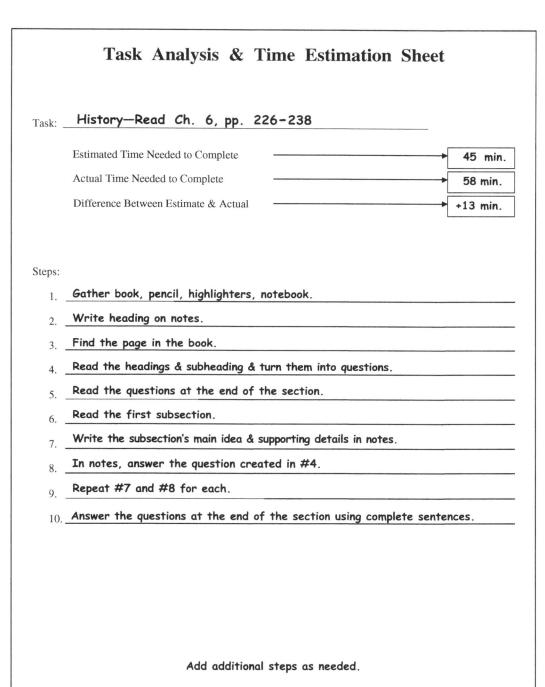

Figure 2. A worksheet for students to develop task analysis and time estimation skills.

> ## Task Analysis and Time Estimation
>
> 1. Set stopwatches to 0:00.
> 2. List all the steps in a task in the correct order.
> 3. Estimate the time to complete the task.
> 4. Prepare to complete the task and start the stopwatch.
> 5. Complete the task.
> 6. Record the actual time to finish the task.
> 7. Calculate the difference between the estimated and actual times.

have three parts. For instance, an assignment to read a chapter and define the vocabulary for a quiz the next day requires students to (a) read, (b) look up words in the dictionary, and (c) identify and remember information likely to be on the quiz. Students unpracticed at task analysis are likely to complete the first and second steps, then assume that the third step will happen on its own. They might do poorly on the quiz even though they believe they did their homework.

Purpose

The purposes of the Task Analysis & Time Estimation Sheet (see Figure 2) are to raise students' awareness of the multiple steps that may be involved in a single task and to develop their perception of how much time it takes to complete that task.

Ideally, teachers should allocate class time over a week or so for students to work with the Task Analysis & Time Estimation Sheets (especially for elementary and middle-school students). If class time is unavailable, teachers can require students to complete the sheets at home and encourage parents or guardians to participate.

Materials

- Kitchen-style timer with a bell
- Stopwatch
- Task Analysis & Time Estimation Sheets

Steps

Teachers first show students how to operate the stopwatch, then ask students to set their stopwatches to 0:00.

Choosing and Analyzing Tasks

Students should start with a basic task, such as making their bed in the morning. Students list all the steps to complete the task in the correct order.

Teachers then have students estimate the time they think it takes to complete the task, noting that students will have a fair idea if the task is routine.

Students next progress to a discrete academic task, such as a homework assignment or chapter reading. They generally need guidance at this point to avoid oversimplifying. For example, for an assignment to read the first section of chapter 6 in their social studies textbook, students might simply write one step — *read* — on their worksheets unless explicitly directed to break the task into smaller steps.

As students begin to grasp the complexity of simple, discrete tasks, teachers can extend task analysis to far more complex tasks, like writing a research paper and preparing for a final examination.

Testing Students' Time Estimates

Once a task is analyzed and its time estimated, students prepare to complete the task and start the stopwatch. When the task is complete, they stop the timer and record the actual time on the worksheet. (Students should stop the timer if they are interrupted or have to stop for more than a minute so their actual times will be accurate.) Last, students calculate how much they under- or overestimated their task time.

As stated, students should use the Task Analysis & Time Estimation Sheet over a week or more. They quickly learn to look at the previous day's actual time to estimate the current day's task time. The activity is helpful to teachers as well as students, as it reveals the wide differences in task-completion times within a class.

Mastering the Routine

Accurately estimating how much time it takes to complete tasks is essential for long-term planning. When students complete Task Analysis & Time Estimation Sheets for a period of time, they learn that their actual times vary according to the length and complexity of the assignment, their level of concentration, and other factors like fatigue, motivation, and interest. They also learn which tasks are quick and easy and which require more time and effort. Students get quite good at this when they practice enough.

After some intensive daily work on task analysis and time estimation, teachers can require students to track estimated and actual time on their daily task list in the strategic calendar system, which is introduced below.

Strategic Calendar System

Purpose

The *strategic calendar system* helps students manage the academic, extracurricular, familial, and work demands on their time. The system encourages students to plan ahead and think flexibly about efficient time management. While there are many viable strategies for setting up, using, and maintaining a strategic calendar system, the approach described here is a straightforward option. One of its benefits is that it combines practice for short- and long-term planning with time estimation.

Materials

The strategic calendar system has three key components. Ideally, all three are bound into one volume.

The *12-month calendar* is a one-page-per-month calendar with days and dates clearly labeled. Students note everything that places demands on their time on this calendar, excluding their daily homework. The calendar provides the structure for students to balance extracurricular activities and family responsibilities with their homework, which goes in the homework assignment book.

> ### The Strategic Calendar System
>
> 1. Write all tasks, obligations, and special circumstances in the 12-month calendar. Transfer all entries to the homework assignment book.
>
> 2. Record homework and estimated time in the homework assignment book. Time homework and note the actual time.
>
> 3. Record all tasks for the next day in the daily schedule and task list. Plan use of time. Compare time estimates for the current day's homework with actual time. Evaluate time management weekly.

The *homework assignment book* is a bound volume with blocks for recording daily homework for each subject and extra space to note other tasks. It should have adequate space for students to write down complete assignments. For example, the book should have enough space for students to record their math homework as "All odds pp. 217–18" rather than just "217" or "problems."

The *daily schedule and task list* provides a set location for students to write down everything they must accomplish in a given day. Students use its time blocks to identify when they will complete each task.

September 2007

Sun	Mon	Tue	Wed	Thu	Fri	Sat
						1
2 Family Trip	3 LABOR DAY	4 Band 7:30-8:30 AM Soccer 6-7	5 First Day of School	6 Band 7:30-8:30 AM Lesson 3-4 Rehearsal 6-8	7	8 Soccer Away 10 AM
9 Sunday School AM Rehearse 2-4	10	11 Band Soccer 6-7	12 Rehearsal 6:30-8	13 Band Trombone Soccer 6-7	14	15 Soccer Away 11 Rehearsal 3-5
16 Sunday School	17 Rehearsal 6:30-8	18 Band Soccer 6-7	19 Rehearsal 6:30-8	20 Band Trombone Soccer 6-7	21	22 Soccer Home 10 Rehearsal 12-5
23 Sunday School TRIP ALL DAY	24	25 Band Soccer 6-7	26	½ DAY! 27 Band No lesson. Rehearsal 6:30-8	28	29 Soccer Away 11
30 Sunday School						

Figure 3. One month from a student's twelve-month calendar.

The Monthly Calendar

Students include everything that puts demands on their time. They exclude activities that are part of their daily routine, such as getting dressed and eating dinner.

Examples

Work schedules
Appointments
Sports practices and games
Meetings
Lessons
Birthdays and anniversaries
Holidays
Vacations
Tests and exams
Essays and projects
Special events

Daily schedules and task lists can be quite informative. Regular use helps students establish routines and make better use of their time. Some students find they have more time than they thought, while others get visual evidence that they are overcommitted. A daily schedule and task list is a good way for students to begin assessing what is reasonable to accomplish.

Steps

Twelve-Month Calendar

At the beginning of the school year, then at least monthly, students write all tasks that put demands on their time in the monthly calendar, plus other obligations or special circumstances that relate to their schedules. When a test, paper, or other project is assigned ahead of time, students note its due date on their calendars. Figure 3 shows a sample month.

Homework Assignment Book

Students transfer all obligations from their monthly calendar to the corresponding dates in the homework assignment book whenever they update their calendars.

On a daily basis, students record their homework and the time they estimate it will take in the assignment notebook. A sample is shown in Figure 4.

Teachers should write the homework in the same place on the board every day and give students time to record it at the beginning of class. If there is no homework, students should write "no hw" or draw a line through the box to prevent uncertainty rather than leave the block blank.

Students then time their homework and note the actual time next to the time they estimated when the assignment was given. They also choose a system for marking off each assignment after they finish it. Whether they cross it out, write a checkmark beside it, or sign it, they get the visual satisfaction of a task completed.

	Monday 9/24	Tuesday 9/25	Wednesday 9/26	Thursday 9/27	Friday 9/28
Estimated Time/ Actual Time	2:40 2:20	1:25 1:30	1:30 1:30	2:35 2:22	1:05 0:45
Math	pp. 56-58 math MJ	pp. 59-60 MJ	pp. 61-63 MJ	Complete practice test and make corrections on pp. 50 - 65 in MJ	Math test Monday Chapter 3
English **History**	Categorize spelling words by rules Read folktale 1 and complete organizer Vocabulary cards pp. 226-238	Read folktale 2 and complete organizer Answer questions in complete sentences p. 238	Read folktale 3 and complete organizer Nothing	Compare/Contrast essay about folktales read in class. Use organizers as guide. Read and take notes pp. 240-250	Nothing Vocabulary cards pp. 240-250
Science **French**	p. 139 answer questions in complete sentences Study greetings sheet for quiz tomorrow.	Complete plants outline None	Lab #2 type and complete conclusion None	p. 156 answer questions in complete sentences None	Correct Lab #2 Review all worksheets for Quiz Tuesday
Music **Health**	Complete Jazz sheet due Wednesday Finish crossword.	Complete Jazz sheet due Wednesday None	None None	None None	None None
Parent Signature /Notes					

Figure 4. **One page from a student's homework assignment book.**

Teachers can check students' homework assignment books on a daily basis or have students check each others' for accuracy. For younger students and students having difficulty using the book, teachers can ask a parent or guardian to check the book every day and sign it.

Daily Schedule and Task List

Figure 5 shows the daily schedule and task list. On a daily basis, students record what they must accomplish the next day and how they will use their time. Students consider daily routines that require time (showering, eating, traveling, etc.), scheduled activities, and time for homework.

TASK LIST	DAILY SCHEDULE	
Day: Thursday **Date:** 9/27/07		
BEFORE SCHOOL		
Shower Eat	**6 AM**	
	6:30	Shower + eat
	7 AM	Travel
	7:30	Band practice
AFTER SCHOOL/EVENING		
Trombone lesson Homework Dinner Play Rehearsal	**2 PM**	
	2:30	in school
	3 PM	snack
	3:30	Trombone Lesson
	4 PM	Travel Home
	4:30	Homework
BEFORE BED	**5 PM**	Homework
Pack backpack + music Brush Teeth Feed Hampster	**5:30**	Eat Dinner
	6 PM	Travel to Rehearsal
	6:30	Rehearsal
Things To Remember	**7 PM**	Rehearsal
$ for trombone lesson trombone	**7:30**	Rehearsal
	8 PM	Travel Home
	8:30	Finish Homework
	9 PM	Bed + Hampster
	9:30	
	10 PM	

Figure 5. One student's daily schedule and task list.

Homework time can vary quite a bit from day to day, as the sample assignment book in figure 4 shows. After students plan their next day using the calendar and daily schedule, they should compare the time estimates they made for the current day's homework with their actual time. They may find that adjustments to their schedules are required.

On a weekly basis, students evaluate the previous week's time management and use the information to plan their coming week using the daily schedule and task list.

Mastering the Routine

Keeping the strategic calendar system up to date is essential. Although students generally enjoy setting it up, most will not

The Daily Schedule and Task List

Problem: Not Enough Hours in the Day!

Robert, a high-school junior, found his grades were dropping, and he was experiencing increased anxiety about school.

Strategy

One day his teacher asked the class to complete a daily schedule for a period of one week. She wanted her class to look critically at how they were using their free time.

Result

Robert's schedule confirmed for him that his job at the convenience store was too much for him to handle in addition to varsity basketball and the choral society. The schedule also made him see that he could do homework during his daily free period instead of going to the cafeteria with his friends.

He gave notice at his job, and told his friends that he was going to work in the library three of the five days. He felt his anxiety ease as he "found" an additional 16 hours each week.

routinely use it unless required to. Routines take time, perseverance, and motivation to establish. In addition to offering class time for students to get organized, teachers can facilitate students' development of time management skills by:

- providing a detailed course or weekly syllabus
- giving plenty of notice about tests, essays, and projects so students can plan accordingly
- soliciting feedback on what tools are working (and are not) and suggestions for improvements

Good teachers listen to students' ideas for changing or adjusting practices in ways that will help them.

In the end, strategic calendar use is a skill students develop throughout their lives, and adapt as they see fit. They may drop one or more tools if they find they can manage with less detail. They may choose electronic calendars instead of paper ones. Or, they may find that this system truly works for them. Students should learn and use one system, however, before they begin to adjust it.

This approach to mastery teaching is basic. When artists are learning to paint, teachers often have them practice and demonstrate mastery of particular techniques for mixing colors or achieving textures. As students develop, they become free to experiment. This strategy equally applies to instruction in music, athletics, penmanship, and other disciplines. As children grow into adulthood, they adjust and adapt what they have learned to meet their needs.

Closing Thoughts on Time Management Skills

Learning to manage time is a little like learning to drive. When we learn to drive we must integrate multiple skills. At first we are focused on using the machinery properly and adjusting to where the car is in space. Before these skills fully develop, they take a great deal of concentration and we often drive too far to the right, drift into another lane, or swipe overhanging branches. The car may stall because we do not properly engage the clutch, or we are startled when the windshield wipers come on instead of the turn signal. Sometimes we have to slam on the brakes or swerve because we are not looking far enough ahead. Not until we have learned to manage the mechanics of the car automatically, focus our eyes on the road, shift our focus to and from the mirrors, and adjust our speed and steering to accommodate what is going on around us do we master the art of driving. Still, surprises come our way. If we have become competent drivers — alert and confident — we can successfully accommodate the unexpected.

Managing time in a way that balances academic, extracurricular, work, and familial responsibilities is not so different. Teachers should encourage students to learn one skill at a time until they master individual routines. Teachers should offer a great deal of support and guidance, as well as many opportunities to practice, before expecting students to integrate skills and be competent learners.

CHAPTER 5

PREREQUISITE COMPREHENSION SKILLS

Introduction

Watch a group of individuals approach an unfamiliar and complex task, and a surprising variety of learning and problem-solving strategies emerge — ranging from shockingly inefficient to amazingly effective. Those who have participated in the New Games challenges developed by Dale LeFevre in the 1970s or the ropes courses run by Outward Bound and other organizations may recall the silence that groups experience in the period between learning about the challenge and generating their first suggestion for approaching it. This period is important to the success of the group because people are working to comprehend the task and generate possible strategies. Ultimately, the individuals who emerge as leaders of the group are those who fully comprehend the complexity of the task and can rally the group to implement the most effective strategies.

Comprehension is a prerequisite for choosing and implementing an effective strategy, yet all too frequently students neither comprehend the material they are supposed to study nor possess effective strategies to aid their understanding. Some students simply give up, slam their book closed and say, "This is stupid!" Others read and reread, hoping the meaning will suddenly become clear. Some depend on the teacher to explain it all, raising their hands to confess "I don't get it." When asked what they don't understand, the response is often "Any of it." Students who do not possess effective strategies highlight entire pages of the textbook, attempt to write down every word that comes out of the teacher's mouth, or resort to rote memorization for the test. Their essays and projects are an amalgam of quotes strung together with a few transitional words that offer little in the way of interpretation and draw no conclusions.

The Case for Teaching Comprehension Strategies

Successfully *studying* a topic means engaging in two cognitive tasks simultaneously: acquiring content and implementing learning strategies. As content becomes more challenging, effective comprehension strategies play an ever-more-essential role. Students who have not been taught strategies for learning content fall behind their peers.

Comprehension skills and study skills have a symbiotic relationship. Each supports and develops the other. Teachers can effectively teach management strategies for information and ideas (covered in chapter 6) only when students can comprehend the sources of information and ideas. Students need to be able to recognize and formulate topics, main ideas, and supporting details to understand and manage content.

Why is teaching comprehension strategies such a difficult problem in the classroom? Most know the catch-22. In the current educational climate in the United States, teachers are expected to cover more content in a shorter time than ever before so their students demonstrate proficiency on state-mandated tests. Essentially, it seems there is no time to teach learning strategies. At the same time, if students are to develop the academic competence to perform well on tests, they need a collection of learning strategies to draw from to fulfill challenging tasks.

To teach comprehension strategies, teachers must reduce the cognitive load on students. They must put aside expectations for new or complex content acquisition and focus on teaching each strategy until students master it. Just as a preschool teacher may offer a frustrated child a puzzle with fewer pieces and teach him or her strategies for putting it together, classroom teachers should give students familiar content and teach them strategies for studying it. Equipped with such strategies, students can approach challenging tasks with increasing confidence and competence.

Rationale, Objectives, and Prerequisites

Learning to recognize text structure and to apply strategies to identify and generate topics, main ideas, and supporting details is essential to developing comprehension skills (as well as written expression skills) and a prerequisite to learning study skills.

The objectives of prerequisite comprehension skills are for students to learn to:

- identify topics
- identify explicitly stated main ideas
- identify supporting details
- infer an implied main idea from suppporting details
- recognize various text structures

To meet these objectives, students should already be able to decode assigned texts and use a dictionary and thesaurus.

Key Comprehension Skills

Categorizing

Purpose

Before students can successfully identify main ideas and details, they need to know how to categorize. The *bucket* (Sedita, 2001) is an effective visual aid and metaphor for teaching students to categorize (Figure 6). In these exercises, students apply categorizing strategies to words and ideas before they learn and apply them to paragraphs and essays.

Teachers begin with basic or concrete categorizing exercises and progress to more advanced or abstract exercises as students advance. Table 2 gives examples for categorizing exercises at the basic (concrete) and more advanced (abstract) levels.

Materials

The most concrete approach to this exercise is to use actual objects — an actual bucket and objects for students to categorize. That means including objects that both fit and do not fit a given category.

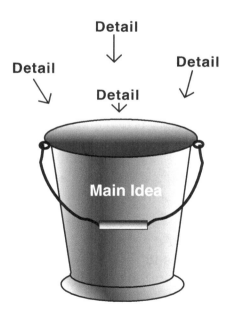

Figure 6. **The bucket helps students learn to identify and distinguish between main ideas and details.**

Table 2. Using the Bucket to Teach Categorizing at Basic and More Advanced Levels		
Level	**Category or Main Idea**	**Possible Contents or Details**
Basic (concrete)	School supplies	• Pens • Pencils • Rulers • Notebooks
Basic (concrete)	Fruit	• Blueberries • Apples • Strawberries • Oranges
Advanced (abstract)	Feelings	• Happiness • Sadness • Anger
Advanced (abstract)	Dictators	• Hitler • Pol Pot • Saddam Hussein

Steps

Teachers introduce categorizing by labeling the bucket with a category (main idea) and asking students to identify contents for the bucket (details) that fit the category. It's best to begin with something familiar. For example, the teacher might label the bucket *beach toys*, and students might fill it with a shovel, a castle mold, a kickboard, a skimboard, and a Frisbee. Anything that may or may not fit in the category is debated by the group and either included or discarded. For example, students might note that a kickboard is usually used in a pool and should be discarded, and a Frisbee can be used in many places other than the beach. Such discussions improve students' critical thinking skills and help them understand that categorizing is not an exact science.

When students understand the concepts underlying categorizing, teachers can choose a more advanced category from students' studies. If students are learning geometric figures in math, for example, teachers might label the bucket *irregular polygons* and ask students to fill the bucket with examples that fit the category.

Once students can provide appropriate components for a category, teachers can give students the contents of the bucket and ask them to provide the label. If students are learning about dependent clauses in English, for example, teachers can provide a number of clauses and ask them to come up with the category *dependent clauses* to label the bucket.

This activity leads to discussions about choosing a label that is not too broad or narrow for the bucket's components. For beach toys, the label toys would be too broad while *water toys* would be too narrow. The story of *Goldilocks and the Three Bears* is helpful here. When Goldilocks wanted a bowl of porridge, she found one bowl was too hot, one was too cold, and one was just right. When she wanted a bed, she found one bed was too hard, one was too soft, and one was just right. The *Goldilocks strategy* (Sedita, 2001) can help students create a label for the bucket that is just right.

Categorizing strategies help develop students' skills in identifying the main idea and supporting details, since the main idea is equivalent to the bucket label and the supporting details are equivalent to the bucket's contents.

Identifying Topics, Main Ideas, and Supporting Details

Purpose

The *topic* is a word or phrase that states the subject of a text (what the text is about). The *main idea* is the point the author is making about the topic. *Supporting details* are pieces of information within the text that elaborate upon and support the main idea. Being able to identify the topic, main idea, and supporting details helps students comprehend what they read and is a prerequisite for taking effective notes.

Materials

Students need a selection of expository paragraphs that explicitly state their main ideas and that students have the skills to decode. Students also need a selection of expository paragraphs in which the main idea is implied by the supporting details.

Texts should be short and concrete when students are first exposed to strategies for identifying topics and main ideas. Only after students demonstrate a solid grasp of the skill should they begin working with longer texts or more challenging content.

> **Identifying Topics, Main Ideas, and Supporting Details**
>
> 1. Identify the topic of a paragraph by looking for words that frequently appear.
>
> 2. Self-question to identify the main idea of the paragraph.
>
> 3. List the details that support or offer more information about the main idea.

Steps

Topic Identification Strategy

Teachers introduce topic identification by explaining the strategy of looking for words (or synonyms and pronouns) that frequently appear in a given paragraph. For example, students can be asked to underline the word (and its synonyms and pronouns) that appears most frequently in the paragraph below, excluding small words such as _a_ and _the_. This leads them to the topic, which is penguins — specifically, Adelie penguins.

> Adelie penguins are adorable. These are the penguins that are shown in most pictures of penguins. Adelies look like little bowling pins wearing tuxedos. They live in large groups in the south polar regions. At times they can be very funny. It is often enjoyable to watch them as they swim or slide in the snow on their bellies. (Vener, 2002, p. 10)

Main Idea Identification Strategy

Once students can identify the topic of a paragraph, they can learn to identify the main idea. Teachers should introduce this strategy using a short paragraph that explicitly states the main idea.

Note that many students have difficulty at this point because they do not fully understand the difference between a main idea and a supporting detail. By implementing the categorizing activities presented earlier, teachers can better prepare students to identify the main idea.

First, teachers should explain the most common forms of paragraph structure that relate to an explicitly stated main idea. Often, the main idea is the first sentence of a paragraph. The writer uses the rest of the paragraph to support the main idea. The next most common placement for the main idea is the last sentence of a paragraph. The author gives supporting information first and then makes the point. Last, main ideas can be located in the middle of a paragraph.

Next, teachers ask students to identify the topic of the given paragraph. In the sample paragraph above, the topic is Adelie penguins.

Teachers then instruct students to self-question to identify the main idea. Students should ask themselves, _What point is the author making about the topic?_ For the sample paragraph above, the main idea is that Adelie penguins are adorable. It is stated in the first sentence. The other sentences provide details that support the main idea; two of the sentences tell us about Adelie penguins, while three give examples of how adorable they are.

Supporting Details Identification Strategy

Once students demonstrate skill at identifying the main idea of a text, supporting details are often easy to identify. They come in a variety of guises, including facts, descriptions, explanations, and examples. Learning to identify supporting details increases comprehension and enhances students' ability to elaborate on their own ideas in expository writing. It is an essential skill.

Teachers should introduce supporting detail identification strategies using a short paragraph that explicitly states the main idea and provides several supporting details. Students first practice identifying the topic of the paragraph, then identifying the main idea, then listing the details that support or offer more information about the main idea.

In the paragraph about Adelie penguins (repeated below), the main idea is Adelie penguins are adorable. Students' next task is to identify details in the paragraph that support the main idea. The supporting details are underlined below.

> Adelie penguins are adorable. These are the penguins that are <u>shown in most pictures of penguins</u>. Adelies <u>look like little bowling pins wearing tuxedos</u>. They live in large groups in the south polar regions. At times they <u>can be very funny</u>. It is often <u>enjoyable to watch them as they swim or slide</u> in the snow on their bellies. (Vener, 2002, p. 10)

Note that the information that Adelie penguins live in large groups in south polar regions is not underlined. Why? This information, while important, does not support the main idea. Extraneous information in a paragraph frustrates students who are learning to identify supporting details. They want to underline it because it is important information, yet it does not support the main idea. Teachers should point out such information so students see the difference between a unified paragraph and one that includes extraneous detail. In the paragraph above, the extraneous detail would be better placed in a separate paragraph about Adelie penguins' habitat.

Identifying an Implied Main Idea Through Supporting Details

Purpose

Many texts do not explicitly state their main idea. Rather, they offer an *implied main idea*, and students are expected to infer it by examining the details in the text. Many students struggle with this inferential thinking skill. It requires students to be able to identify both the topic and supporting details. Revisiting the categorizing activities presented earlier in this chapter can be helpful at this point; identifying implied main ideas is similar to labeling the bucket.

Identifying an Implied Main Idea Through Supporting Details

1. Identify the topic of a paragraph.

2. Apply the main idea identification strategy.

3. Use supporting details to identify the implied main idea.

Materials

Students need a selection of paragraphs that imply the main idea and that they have the skill to decode.

Steps

Teachers should first explain the words *imply* and *infer*, then provide students with a paragraph in which the main idea is implied. Students identify the topic of the paragraph by underlining the words that appear most frequently. In the sample paragraph below, the topic is Sam and the play.

> Sam was up for most of the night before the play. He went over the lines again and again in his head. He was sure that he knew them all; still he could not help but wonder what it would be like if he forgot his lines in front of all those people. He knew that he needed a good night's sleep if he was to be refreshed and ready for the play the next evening. Still he tossed and turned. (Vener, 2002, p. 32)

Next, students apply the main idea identification strategy to see if the main idea is explicitly stated or implied. What is the main idea? Is it stated? Or, do the details add up for students to figure it out?

In the paragraph above, some students will identify the first sentence as the stated main idea. However, the author's point is to help us understand *why* Sam was up most of the night before the play. The supporting details (including the first sentence) all contribute to make the author's point. We are told that:

- Sam was up for most of the night before the play.
- Sam is sure he knows his lines, but he keeps practicing them anyway.
- Sam wonders what will happen if he forgets his lines in front of the audience.
- Sam knows he needs a good night's sleep, but he tosses and turns.

What point is the author making? Students can infer from the details in the paragraph that Sam is nervous. Therefore, the implied main idea is that Sam is nervous about the play.

Mastering the Skills of Categorizing and Identifying Topics, Main Ideas, and Supporting Details

Once students can categorize, and identify topics, main ideas, and supporting details in single, concrete paragraphs, teachers may progress in one of two directions: to single paragraphs with more abstract ideas or to longer selections that remain at the basic or concrete level.

The transition to longer selections with multiple paragraphs tends to confuse students. They must first be taught that an essay, for example, has one overarching main idea or thesis that is stated in the first paragraph. The thesis is then supported by subsequent paragraphs, each with its own main idea and supporting details. It is well worth taking the time to explain and model this structure. Figure 7 is useful for this purpose.

Closing Thoughts on Prerequisite Comprehension Skills refers to the ways in which we link sentences into paragraphs and paragraphs into essays. The expository structure of main idea or thesis, supporting details, and conclusion can be unfamiliar and unwieldy to students whose oral discourse is generally narrative in structure. Once teachers show students how expository prose is structured and the different forms it can take, they can more easily comprehend and participate in the academic discourse that begins around middle school and continues throughout their formal education and beyond.

Just as languages have accepted rules of syntax within sentences, academic discourse has commonly accepted forms and structures within paragraphs and essays. Most academic expository texts follow a general three-part structure. The first part is introductory or background information that culminates in an explicit or implied main idea (the thesis). The second part presents evidence to support or explain the main idea or thesis. The third part offers concluding material that summarizes the most important points, states the significance of the main idea or thesis, and either explicitly or implicitly calls for some sort of response.

The form an author uses contributes to the text's intended meaning and purpose. For example, a comparison of two types of tennis raquets might present the same information as a straightforward description of each, but organize the information differently. The writer might compare the quality of the components of the two brands rather than give a full, holistic description of each type of raquet.

A clear understanding of the structure of expository discourse in its various manifestations (e.g., textbooks, editorials, book reviews, interviews, profiles, and reporting) and forms (summarizing, describing, comparing, contrasting, and persuading) is essential for students to be successful in school. The best way to create this understanding is to teach the forms and structures explicitly, sequentially, and with many opportunities for students to identify types of expository text as well as to practice writing it.

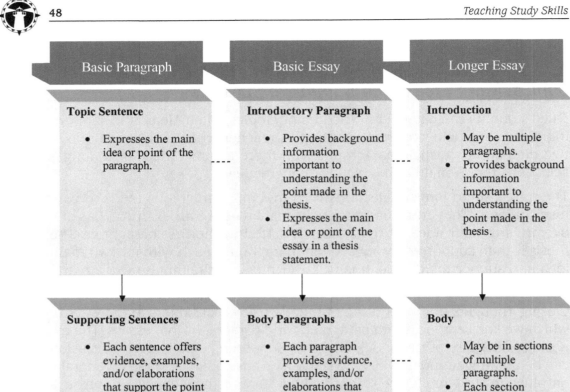

Figure 7. **Paragraph and essay structure.**

The most effective method for helping students develop discourse skills is practice. Students need regular practice in recognizing the forms of discourse in what they read, see, and hear. They also need constant practice generating their own discourse in paragraphs, essays, speeches, and multimedia projects.

CHAPTER 6

MANAGING INFORMATION AND IDEAS

Introduction

By adulthood, most of us have developed strategies to filter and organize the barrage of information and ideas we encounter every day. We've learned to skim the headlines of the news, reading more closely for developments in our particular areas of interest. We listen to friends, family, and colleagues, automatically sorting information and ideas we want to remember and prioritizing and planning appropriate responses. We know we cannot understand and remember everything, so we focus on the topics that interest us or are necessary to improve our professional and personal lives. We develop a core base of knowledge and add to that core each time we experience something that relates to it.

Strategies for filtering and organizing information are developed and honed in school, and are particularly essential to academic success. At no other time in our lives are we expected to take in, remember, and demonstrate mastery of such a wide range of information from so many fields of study. The information management strategies students need extend from highlighting the main idea of a paragraph to preparing for a comprehensive final examination.

Many students struggle to acquire effective strategies for managing information. They need explicit instruction and ongoing guided practice if they are to succeed in organizing and remembering all that is required of them. The reasons for their struggles vary widely. As the student profiles in earlier chapters attest, students may lack motivation, opportunities to learn and practice, or basic skills. A shortage of basic skills is the case for most students.

Student Profiles

Merima

In class, Merima listens to the teacher and enthusiastically participates in discussions and projects. She likes learning about new topics and asks many questions. On her most recent progress report, however, her teachers commented that her enthusiasm did not compensate for her failing grades on several tests. Merima says she understands everything when it is presented in class, but cannot seem to remember it during the test.

Merima's books and notebooks are filled with notes to friends and intricate drawings. Merima explains that she does not take notes in class because most of the teachers provide handouts with all the information on them. To study for her tests, she "looks through the handouts."

Merima needs teachers to hold her accountable for taking notes in class and preparing a study guide prior to tests. While teachers might provide a handout for particularly dense material, the process of taking class notes and summarizing those notes in preparation for tests ensures that information and ideas are more firmly imprinted in memory. Merima would benefit from having teachers who monitor her during this process and work with her to compare her past performance on tests with how she performs when she implements note-taking and study strategies.

Angel

Angel learned some very effective study strategies in middle school but feels frustrated in his new high school. He is not allowed to write in his books, so he cannot highlight or take notes in the margins. In fact, he is not allowed to take his books home because they are shared by several classes. His teachers give lectures daily, but they write only a few words on the board and speak quickly. Angel has noticed that ideas from class discussions end up on the tests, but he doesn't often get them into his notes because he has difficulty hearing what students on the other side of the room are saying.

Angel would benefit from owning his books so he can mark them up and study from them. He needs teachers who speak slowly enough for students to take competent notes and, ideally, write the essential ideas on the board. He also needs teachers who recognize the difficulty of taking notes from class discussions. Such teachers repeat students' questions and comments so that everyone in the class can hear, as well as point out particularly relevant comments.

Adofo

Adofo keeps his materials carefully organized and completes all his work on time. He tries very hard to do everything his teachers tell him to do: he owns his textbooks, highlights his reading assignments, writes down everything they put on the board, and frequently asks teachers to repeat what they said so he can get the information into his notes. On most nights, Adofo copies over his class notes so they are neat and readable.

Yet, Adofo performs poorly on essays and tests that require him to do more than recognize the correct answer from multiple-choice, matching, or true/false questions — surprising his teachers and parents. Adofo seems to be doing all the right things, but he is not succeeding. A look at Adofo's textbooks shows that he has not learned how to highlight effectively; more than half of each page is highlighted. He explains that he highlights "whatever I don't know" as he reads along. His class notes, although neat, are written across the entire page and in complete sentences. The sentences quote what his teachers have written or said in class. When asked how he prepares for tests, he explains that he "memorizes everything."

Adofo needs teachers to help him develop more efficient highlighting and note-taking skills. He also needs to learn to create study guides, which will encourage him to move beyond rote memory of facts to making connections among main ideas.

Merima, Angel, and Adofo are serious students who care about succeeding in school and make their best efforts, but still struggle. They need teachers who can offer explicit instruction and ongoing opportunities to develop and hone necessary skills to the point of efficiency. They also need teachers who can help them see the connection between effective study skills and success on tests and other projects.

Teaching Information Management

Information management strategies contribute to students' competence and confidence. They enhance comprehension of content by requiring students to read, listen, and learn actively. They also develop students' academic confidence, or self-efficacy — the belief that our actions lead to success. As stated in chapter 1, self-efficacy is essential to academic competence.

There are scores of strategies for teaching students to manage the vast array of information and ideas they must learn to succeed in school. As with all study skills, these strategies must be explicitly taught in a highly structured, sequential manner and practiced with teachers' guidance. Too frequently, teachers ask students to apply study strategies, such as taking notes and writing summaries, when students have never learned them.

This chapter presents strategies discretely to underscore the importance of teaching one strategy at a time, in sequence. Once students learn, practice, and demonstrate mastery of each strategy in isolation, they can begin to use and combine the strategies independently, selecting those that most empower them to understand and remember important information and ideas. Students' ability to select select appropriate strategies for specific tasks is key, as employing all the strategies for a single reading assignment would be highly inefficient.

When students are first learning a study strategy, they should work with familiar information and ideas so they can focus on the strategy without having to allocate much attention to understanding the content. Teachers should teach highlighting, for example, using a chapter students have already studied. Once students master the strategy using known information, they can practice on less familiar topics. Ultimately, the goal is for students to learn to use the strategy independently to master new information.

Rationale, Objectives, and Prerequisites

Information management skills allow students to organize vast amounts of information into logical categories. Students use these categories as a starting point for higher order thinking skills (such as deducing ideas, patterns, and themes), integrating new information and ideas with existing knowledge, and synthesizing and generalizing new information and ideas.

The objectives of information management skills are for students to learn to:

- highlight
- take notes from written sources
- paraphrase
- summarize
- prepare a study guide

To meet these objectives, students should already be able to decode assigned texts, use a dictionary and thesaurus, and identify main ideas and supporting details.

SQ3R

Purpose

SQ3R is a popular study strategy that promotes active reading. Developed by Francis P. Robinson and introduced in 1946, SQ3R describes a five-step process: survey, question, read, recite, review. Although the strategy lacks a solid research base demonstrating measurable effectiveness, it is a useful pneumonic that reminds students to preview a reading assignment and become familiar with the topic (survey), prime themselves to identify main ideas (question), read actively to gain understanding (read and recite), and file new information and ideas into memory (review).

A step-by-step process for approaching a reading assignment can prevent students from becoming overwhelmed by large amounts of new information and encourage them to develop active reading routines. An effective approach to teaching SQ3R is to preview the steps at the beginning of the school year, then match each step with complementary study strategies as they are introduced. The survey step, for example, corresponds to identifying a text's form and structure, which was discussed in chapter 5. The question, read, and recite steps correlate with strategies for identifying the main idea, highlighting, and note-taking. The review step correlates with paraphrasing, summarizing, and creating study guides.

Table 3 outlines the steps of SQ3R. In this chapter, each step is further developed within the purview of other information management strategies.

Highlighting (Expository Text)

Purpose

Highlighting is an active reading strategy. It requires students to mark main ideas and essential supporting details. When explicitly taught, highlighting can be very useful in building students' comprehension. It helps students take notes, summarize, and locate information in the text.

As described in chapter 5, identifying main ideas and supporting details is a reading comprehension skill, and should be explicitly taught before or while teaching highlighting. Highlighting itself is a study strategy — an efficient way for students to stay focused and make it easy to refer back to important information and ideas. To focus student learning on this study strategy (rather than comprehension skills), teachers should select reading material that students can both decode and comprehend while learning to highlight.

> ## Highlighting
> 1. Skim the reading selection.
> 2. Reread the selection more closely to identify main ideas and supporting details.
> 3. Highlight the main idea in one color and supporting details in another color.

It is a good idea for teachers to highlight material themselves before presenting it in class. Sometimes teachers present a rule (e.g., every paragraph should have a main idea), and the assignment proves to be an exception. Newpaper and magazine articles, for example, often have paragraphs of one or two sentences that do not offer a main idea.

Table 3. SQ3R: An Outline of the Steps	
SQ3R Step	**Actions**
• **S**urvey	• Read the title of the selection. • Skim the introduction or first few paragraphs. • Read any headings and the first sentence that follows them. • Look at the visuals and read the captions. • Notice how many pages are in the chapter. • Notice any vocabulary words and read them. • Check for end-of-chapter questions and read them. • Check for a summary and read it. • Notice any other unique things about the chapter.

• **Q**uestion	• Change the title (and headings) into questions using these cue words: who, what, when, where, why, how.
	  • For example, "Adoptive Mother Releases Ducklings in the Wild" might become, *Why did the mother release the ducklings?*
	  • This step is easier when the reading has a heading for each section.

• **R**ead	• Read the text actively by looking for the answers to the questions crafted in the question step.

• **R**ecite	• Answer the questions from the question step, plus any questions at the end of the text.
	  • Ideally, students should not quote the text to answer the questions; an accurate paraphrase indicates stronger comprehension.
	  • Teachers should create opportunities for students to apply their newly acquired knowledge and skills to novel situations.

• **R**eview	• Summarize the reading assignment, making sure to include all the main ideas.

Materials

Students need a short expository text they can easily decode and understand, especially when first learning to highlight. A subsection from a textbook chapter or a newspaper editorial on a familiar topic are good places to begin.

Students also need two different color highlighters. One color is to highlight main ideas and the other is to highlight supporting details. Students should use each color consistently for the reading assignment, and ideally throughout the school year

Steps

Teachers should explain that highlighting is a strategy for calling attention to main ideas and supporting details.

Students first skim the reading selection to glean its overall purpose and structure. For example, is the text describing, explaining, comparing, or persuading? This action correlates with surveying in SQ3R.

Students then reread the selection more closely, paragraph by paragraph, to identify main ideas and supporting details. If the selection has a title, students can turn it into a question to help identify the main idea of the selection. If it has section headings (as in textbooks), students can turn these into questions to help identify the main idea of each section. This process corresponds to the questioning step in SQ3R.

As they read each paragraph, students should highlight the main idea in one color and supporting details in the other color. This process corresponds to the reciting step in SQ3R.

Mastering the Routine

Highlighting creates a visual and kinesthetic engagement with the text. The requirement to highlight is a reminder to read with purpose. Highlighting quickly shows teachers if a student can identify and distinguish between main ideas and supporting details.

Highlighting also serves as a stepping stone to more advanced study skills, such as taking margin notes. As students learn and master margin notes, some discard color-coded highlighting, as margin notes are faster and ultimately more useful as a reference. Other students find highlighting so useful that they continue using it with margin notes through their postsecondary studies.

As with every other strategy, the key to mastering the routine is to make it habitual. Students need to know what they are supposed to do, be asked to do it often and consistently, have their work checked, and receive feedback.

Note-Taking from Text Sources

Purpose

Note-taking from written and oral sources is an active reading and listening activity. Notes provide students with rich material to aid in information recall, essay-writing, and exam preparation.

> ## Note-Taking from Text Sources
>
> 1. Write heading on the front: name, date, and topic.
>
> 2. Label the left column on the front *Main Ideas* and the right column *Supporting Details*. Label the left column on the back *Questions* and the right column *Answers*.
>
> 3. Write down the topic.
>
> 4. Copy the highlighted main idea under *Main Ideas* and the highlighted details under *Supporting Details*.
>
> 5. Record questions in under *Questions* on the back.
>
> 6. Ask questions and record correct responses under *Answers*.
>
> 7. Write a summary of the main ideas.

Materials

The two-column, one-sided method of note-taking (see Figures 8 and 9) calls for lined paper, preferably with a wide left margin. (Students can also fold their paper.) Students also need pencils or pens.

Steps

Teachers should provide an example of two-column notes from a written source. The class uses it as a model to discuss how this form of note-taking differs from other forms and how it might be helpful for studying.

Students use headings to keep their notes organized and sequential. The heading on the front includes the student's name, the date, and the topic. The left column is labeled *Main Ideas* and the right column *Supporting Details*. Students only take notes on the front.

The back of each note-taking sheet is reserved for asking questions about the material on the front, and recording answers. Students label the left column on the back *Questions* and the right column *Answers*.

If the class has been learning highlighting, students can practice taking notes using a selection they already highlighted. This is an effective way to help students connect disparate study skills. After they write down the topic, students simply copy the highlighted main idea into the left column of their notes and the highlighted supporting details into the right column. For better visual organization, students should skip a line or two between main ideas and between groups of supporting details.

John Newhall
September 18, 2007
Language Arts

Topic: Sentence Structure	
Main Ideas	Supporting Details
<u>Simple sentence</u>	• Can have one subject + one verb (simple subject SS and simple verb SV)
• Also called <u>independent clause</u>	
• Expresses one complete thought.	• Can have more than one subject and more than one verb (compound subject CS and compound verb CV)
• Must include at least one subject and at least one verb	
	• Ex. Harry runs.
	• SS = Harry; SV = runs
	• Ex. Harry and Natasha run and shout.
	• CS = Harry and Natasha; CV = run and shout
<u>Compound sentence</u>	
• Two+ simple sentences (independent clauses) linked by a comma + coordinating conjunction	• Can have simple or compound subjects and simple or compound verbs
	• Ex. Harry runs, but Jamal walks.
• Can also link independent clauses with	• SS1 = Harry; SS2 = Jamal; SV1 = runs; SV2 = walks
• a semicolon	
• a semicolon + conjunctive adverb + comma	• Ex. Harry and Natasha run and shout, but Jamal and Alicia walk and talk.
	• CS1 = Harry and Natasha; CS2 = Jamal and Alicia; CV1 = run and shout; CV2 = walk and talk

Figure 8. An example of two-column notes (front).

Questions	Answers
Is there a name for a sentence that doesn't express a complete thought?	Sentence fragment
Why is "Clean up your room" an independent clause?	In an imperative sentence (a command), the subject "you" is meant to be understood by the listener, even if it isn't spoken or written.

Summary

The first two types of sentences that are important to know are simple and compound. A simple sentence is called an independent clause. It must have at least one subject and verb and express a complete thought. One subject is called a simple subject, but more than one is called a compound subject. One verb is called a simple verb, but more than one is called a compound verb.

A compound sentence is two simple sentences put together into one. To do this, you have to use a comma plus a coordinating conjunction (or a semicolon, or a semicolon plus a conjunctive adverb plus a comma) between the two simple sentences. A good way to remember the difference is that simple equals one, and compound equals more than one.

Figure 9. An example of two-column notes (back).

If students do not have a highlighted text to work from, teachers can distribute a short expository text for practice. Simple is best. The text should be accessible to all students in terms of decoding level and the complexity of ideas. As teachers read the text with the class, they should "speak" their thought process. For example, "I've read the first few sentences, and the article seems to be about the Civil War, so I think I'll put that at the top of my page as the topic." Teachers then review how to identify main ideas and supporting details and demonstrate how to transfer them to the note-taking sheet. The class then collaborates to read the entire selection and take notes, and reads over the completed notes together.

Next, teachers have students record their questions about the selection in the left column on the back of their note-taking sheet. Students ask their questions to the teacher or the class and record the correct responses in the right column. Students who did not realize they had questions benefit particularly from this exercise, as it adds to their understanding. It is also a good time to alert students to questions that are likely to appear on a test.

Once students finish their notes, they write a summary of the main ideas. (Summarizing is covered later in this chapter.) The summary may be written on the back of the last sheet of notes if there is space or on a separate sheet with the topic clearly identified.

Mastering the Routine

Mastering note-taking takes ongoing guidance from teachers and regular practice. As students progress in school, reading material becomes longer, more difficult to decode, and more complex. Note-taking also becomes more challenging. However, like any skill, practice breeds confidence and ability. The best way to help students master note-taking is to teach them how to do it, build in daily practice, and increase the complexity as students progress. Letting students use their notes for a test is an excellent motivator, as it allows them to see the direct link between mastery of the skill and performance on the assessment.

Note-Taking from Nontext Sources

Purpose

Note-taking from nontext sources (such as lectures and videos) is an essential academic skill, particularly in high school and college, when content from written sources generally becomes secondary to information and ideas presented in class lectures, discussions, and activities. Students use the same note-taking model they use for written sources, but some aspects differ slightly.

Materials

To learn to take notes from nontext sources, students need:

- two-column notepaper and pens or pencils
- short expository films (many are available on the Web, including minidocumentaries, segments of television news shows, and videotaped interviews)
- short recorded audio lectures
- short live lectures

Steps

A good way to begin teaching note-taking from nonprint sources is to use short, highly structured lectures, recorded lectures, and documentary films. Teachers should give students partially completed two-column notes beforehand. The notes should provide the main ideas of the lecture; students then listen for the details and fill them in where they belong. Once students become adept at this process, teachers can offer notes with the details filled in and instruct students to supply the main ideas. As students become increasingly proficient at filling in the missing items, teachers can help them transition to recording main ideas and details independently.

As students gain proficiency, teachers can call their attention to cue words and phrases that can guide their note-taking. Good lecturers generally introduce a lecture with an overview of the main points. For example, a teacher might begin with, "Today we are going to focus on *three stages of seed development*." This opening cues students to listen for the three stages of seed development — formation, growth, and maturation — which are the three main ideas of the lecture. If students can write these main ideas down, they are better prepared to listen for and note the supporting details associated with each stage of seed development. Writing the main points down also helps students track the progress of the lecture.

In addition to previewing their main points, effective lecturers generally punctuate what they say with cue words and phrases intended to capture the audience's attention and provide structure. Students should try to match their notes to the lecture's structure. The lecturer might say, "There are many fascinating details *about the growth stage of seeds*, but *what is most important to understand is ....*" The italicized words in this example alert students to two things: first, their notes should be associated with the growth stage of seeds (the second main idea) and second, the information the speaker is about to impart must be in their notes. As students learn and practice note-taking from lectures or discussions, teachers should routinely call their attention to such cue words and phrases.

Last, good lecturers usually summarize their main points and draw conclusions at the end of the lecture. Students should check that their notes include the points in the lecturer's summary as well as the conclusions.

Mastering the Routine

Abbreviating words contributes to effective note-taking. Many students are unfamiliar with the conventions of abbreviation and benefit from learning even a few. There are scores of abbreviations that, used consistently, decrease the amount of writing students must do. For example, a plus sign (+) can be used to stand for *also, in addition to*, or *another*. The symbol for *therefore* (∴) is also helpful. A Web search will turn up many more useful abbreviations.

Striving to be economical in the use of words is another way to enhance note-taking. Students often feel they need to write down every word of a lecture, when getting the ideas down in as few words as possible is the goal. Teachers can show students how to be economical by omitting small words, such as *a* and *the*.

As an exercise, teachers can have students rewrite their class notes using abbreviations and omitting unnecessary words. The challenge is for students to see how short they can make their notes without losing the essential content.

As with note-taking from text sources, it is highly motivating to let students use their notes from a nonprint source for a test and see the direct link between mastery of the skill and performance on the assessment.

Paraphrasing

Purpose

Paraphrasing means restating or rewriting material using different words and sentence structure than the original. A paraphrase retains all the details of the original (unlike a summary). In addition to the benefit of increasing vocabulary and flexibility with syntax, there are several excellent reasons to teach paraphrasing. It:

- aids comprehension
- imprints information and ideas in memory more solidly
- helps students avoid stringing quotations together in research-based essays
- empowers students to help other people understand material

We paraphrase information on a regular basis without even knowing it, and teachers should call students' attention to this. Telling a joke, explaining homework instructions, and rephrasing the answer to a question are all examples of paraphrasing.

Paraphrasing

1. Replace words or phrases in the source material with synonyms or synonymous phrases (semantic step).

2. Change the structure of the original material without changing its meaning (syntactic step).

3. Combine the semantic and syntactic steps.

Materials

To learn paraphrasing, students need sentences to practice with and a dictionary and thesaurus aimed at their decoding level.

Steps

Teaching paraphrasing is a two-step process. The first step is the *semantic step*. Students replace words or phrases in the source material with accurate synonyms or synonymous phrases. While students may use a thesaurus, this practice can be confusing because synonyms often do not match the context of the original word or phrase. At the beginning, then, it is best to teach paraphrasing by using sentences with familiar vocabulary.

The second step is the *syntactic step*. Once students can replace words and phrases with appropriate synonyms, they practice altering the structure of the original material without changing its meaning.

Students should become proficient at the semantic and syntactic steps separately before teachers guide them to combine the steps.

Paraphrasing correlates to the recite step of SQ3R. Stating information and ideas in different words (as opposed to parroting the words of the text or the teacher) confirms comprehension and ensures that students encode the information in long-term memory.

Mastering the Routine

Students have the most difficulty when they are asked to paraphrase material they do not understand. This is why it is so important to teach the strategy with familiar content before asking students to paraphrase more challenging material. Students should also understand that paraphrasing is an excellent way to check their comprehension.

Paraphrasing Activity

A three-step paraphrasing activity for students is specified in Figure 10. Correct responses appear in italics at the end of each step.

Paraphrasing

Step 1: The Semantic Step

Directions: Exchange each underlined word or phrase with a word or phrase that means the same (synonym). [Many students need assistance with selecting words or phrases to replace with synonyms.]

Sharon <u>is</u> <u>really mad</u> at John because he <u>broke up with her</u>.

Sharon <u>feels</u> <u>extremely angry</u> with John because <u>he ended their relationship</u>.

Step 2: The Syntactic Step

Directions: Change the structure of the sentence below (if possible) by doing one or more of the following:
- changing the order of the words within the sentence
- breaking a compound or complex sentence into simple sentences
- combining simple sentences into a compound or complex sentence

[Many students need assistance to change the sentence structure without losing the original meaning of the sentence.]

Although Sharon only meant to help John improve his looks when she suggested that he should shave off his goatee, he felt hurt and insulted.

Sharon only meant to help John improve his looks. She suggested that he should shave off his goatee. He felt hurt and insulted.

-or-

He felt hurt and insulted when Sharon suggested that he should shave off his goatee even though she only meant to help him improve his looks.

Step 3: 1 + 2 = 3

Directions: Complete the semantic and syntactic steps for the following sentence:

John told Sharon she was an "insensitive cow" and he didn't want to go out with her anymore.

John broke up with Sharon, telling her that she was cold-hearted.

Figure 10. A three-step paraphrasing activity.

Summarizing

Purpose

A *summary* is a short written or oral overview of a topic's main ideas and supporting details. Like paraphrasing, summarizing is an effective way to ensure that students comprehend material. Generating a summary also ensures that students encode the material into long-term memory.

Summarizing Using Two-Column Notes
1. Write a topic sentence.
2. Turn the main ideas in the left column into sentences that include supporting details from the right column.
3. Write a concluding sentence.

Materials

Students need completed two-column notes for the text they will summarize, with the topic, main ideas, and supporting details identified.

Steps

Teachers should first show students an example of a good summary. An effective strategy is for teachers to write a summary of a selection for which students have already taken two-column notes. Teachers can use their model summary to explain the steps for writing a summary, as well as to review paragraph structure.

Students begin practicing the skill using familiar material. Teachers select a well-done set of two-column notes (either their own from a text students know or a student's) and give each student a copy. Together, the class generates a topic sentence for the summary. The class then works together to turn the main ideas in the left column into sentences that include supporting details from the right column. Last, the class generates a concluding sentence for the summary. (Figure 9 shows a sample summary generated from notes.)

Once the class has practiced together several times, students can practice independently. Summarizing correlates to the review step of SQ3R and helps students encode the information and ideas into long-term memory.

Mastering the Routine

Students quickly realize the benefits of taking thorough, neat notes using the divided-sheet format. They also find that writing a summary from their notes often raises additional questions about the topic. Once students have a collection of summaries on a topic, they can engage in critical thinking about ideas related to that topic.

Eventually, students become ready to move directly from reading a text to summarizing it, skipping the highlighting and note-taking steps. However, their readiness depends on their comprehension skills. In other words, students' ability to identify main ideas and supporting details to comprehend a text helps determine their progress at the study skill of summarizing (as well as highlighting and note-taking).

The processes of identifying main ideas and supporting details, taking notes, paraphrasing, and summarizing ensure that students appropriately store information and ideas in memory. Students can then access information and ideas to make connections with existing knowledge, predict outcomes, analyze implications, and critique ideas.

Creating a Study Guide

Purpose

Preparing for a test is often difficult for students who lack strategies to organize and remember information and concepts. If students learn and consistently practice the strategies presented in this guide, however, they are preparing for a test from the first day of a unit of study. Preparing a study guide is simply the logical conclusion of all their work.

Teaching students to prepare a study guide for a content unit or final examination makes them active reviewers and more successful test-takers. Preparing a study guide requires students to collect, organize, and review their work from a period of time. Students who keep portfolios of their work benefit immensely from this practice.

Materials

To create a study guide, students need:

- 12-month calendar
- homework assignment notebook
- daily schedule and task list
- notes and summaries from class and readings, handouts, texts, and other learning materials

Steps

Teachers should help students create a study guide well in advance of a unit test. They should also encourage students to use the strategic calendar system (see chapter 4) to help them plan their study time.

To begin, students arrange all their class notes, homework, handouts, and quizzes that relate to the test in chronological order. When students are first learning, teachers can replace any missing elements, as a thorough study guide requires complete materials. In time, replacing missing elements becomes the student's responsibility.

Students then review all the materials, paying attention to the types of questions asked on earlier quizzes and tests and in class during lectures and discussions.

After the review, teachers instruct students to create a unit summary sheet. The sheet includes:

- student's name and subject

- unit title and dates the unit review packet covers

- main ideas of the unit

- a written summary (or condensed outline) of the main ideas and significant details of the unit

- important vocabulary terms

- questions to ask the teacher during review

- questions likely to be asked on the test

Figure 11 shows a sample unit summary sheet. Teachers then guide students to use the strategic calendar system to plan and schedule their study time.

John Newhall
October 15, 2007
Language Arts

Unit: Sentence Structure   Dates: September 4-October 15, 2007

Main Ideas

• The basic elements of a sentence are the subject and the verb.

• There are four types of sentence structure: simple, compound, complex & compound-complex.

• Each structure has rules for how to use punctuation.

Summary/Outline

simple sentence/independent clause

• a simple or compound subject + simple or compound verb = complete thought

compound sentence

• independent clause + ; + independent clause = compound sentence

• independent clause + , + coordinating conjuction + independent clause = compound sentence

• independent clause + ; + conjunctive adverb + , + independent clause = compound sentence

complex sentence

• independent clause + dependent/subordinate clause = complex sentence

• dependent/subordinate clause + , + independent clause = complex sentence

compound-complex sentence

• two or more independent clauses linked with two or more dependent/subordinate clauses using correct punctuation. Example: Although I hate studying for tests like this, I know I have to do it; if I procrastinate, I'll fail the test.

Vocabulary

Independent clause	Simple subject/verb
Dependent clause	Compound subject/verb
Fragment	Coordinating conjunction
Run-On	Subordinating conjunction

Figure 11. **Sample unit summary sheet.**

Questions Likely To Be on Test

- ID all the vocabulary words
- Label clauses, subjects, and verbs in sentences
- Correct incorrect sentences; make fragments into complete sentences; correct runons
- Write different types of sentences

My Questions

What is the difference between a subordinating conjunction and a conjunctive adverb?

How do I decide when to use a semicolon vs. a coordinating conjunction vs. a conjunctive adverb?

Figure 11. (*cont'd*): Sample unit summary sheet.

Mastering the Routine

Study guide preparation requires teacher-imposed expectations and structure at the beginning. With a consistent and predictable process, however, students begin to understand what is expected of them. Teachers can retain their expectations without providing quite as much structure. Teachers can motivate students to create study guides by making the guide itself the equivalent of a test grade or allowing students to use their study guide to take the test.

Teachers who want students to evaluate their own progress and set goals for future accomplishments can also add a self-evaluation worksheet to the study guide. Figures 12 and 13 provide two samples of self-evaluation. The worksheets ask students to assess their effort and the quality of their work and to set goals for the next unit.

John Newhall
October 22, 2007
Language Arts

Test Analysis

The purpose of the test analysis sheet is to discover where and why you had difficulty on the test and to set goals to improve your test taking skills for the next test.

STEP ONE:
Complete the following chart to see what types of questions are the most difficult for you.

Section of Test / Question Type	Possible Points	Points Earned	Difference
Identifications	20	18	- 2
Editing Fragments	20	20	0
Editing Run- ons	20	14	- 6
Writing Sentence Types	40	20	- 20

STEP TWO:
Determine what to do differently when reviewing for the next test. Examine the questions on which you lost points and find the reason you lost points. Calculate how many points were lost for each reason below:

Reason Deducted	Question (#)	Points
Did not follow directions		
Did not know the answer, but it was in my notes	4, 22, 25, 26	8
Did not know the answer, was not in my notes		
Answer was incomplete; More information needed		
Other(be specific) I didn't check very carefully	32, 34 - 37	20

STEP THREE:
Below, write 2 goals to help you do better on the next test:

1.   I will take some practice tests and have someone check them.
2.   Make sure I ask for help on things I don't understand.

Designed by Brigitta Allen, Landmark School, Inc.

Figure 12. Sample self-evaluation worksheet.

Teachers can also provide students with a more open-ended format for self-evaluation, one that calls on them to think critically about their performance.

John Newhall
October 22, 2007
Language Arts

Self-Evaluation Form for: **Sentence Structure**

How did you study for this test?
First, I made a study guide the week before the test. Then I asked questions about the things I didn't understand. I wrote notes about them on my study guide. I studied the study guide on two nights before the test by reading over it. Finally, I asked my mom to quiz me.

Did you put a lot of effort into making the study guide?
Yes. But it was frustrating because I was absent for two days and missed some of the notes. I got them from Ben, but I still didn't understand some of the stuff I missed.

What was easy for you on the test?
The definitions and fixing sentence fragments.

What was difficult for you on the test?
Fixing run-on sentences the right way and writing different types of sentences. I still don't get compound-complex sentences.

How will you change your study plan for the next test?
Instead of just memorizing the definitions, I will practice fixing sentences and writing different kinds of sentences. I like doing the study guide because it made me get all my notes organized. I should come for extra help to make sure I understand the stuff that is hard for me.

Figure 13. **Sample test reflection sheet.**

Closing Thoughts on Information Management

Developing effective strategies for managing information and ideas is a complex process that requires efficient coordination of multiple neurological networks. Taking notes from a lecture, for example, is successful only when the student can arrive at the lecture on time; find a pen and paper; focus and sustain attention; hear, process, and comprehend the auditory input; select relevant information to write down; take legible notes; and file the notes in an accessible place. Each of these subtasks requires the marshalling of various procedural, intellectual, and emotional connections in the brain. Discretely, the subtasks are complicated enough and cause tremendous difficulty for many students. Together, they comprise a Herculean task of precise coordination to produce the desired result.

This task is carried out by the brain's executive function. As stated in chapter 1, Brown (2007) provides a useful analogy by likening the brain to a symphony orchestra and the brain's executive function to the conductor. Many students struggle in school because the musicians in their orchestras are untrained and their conductors are overwhelmed.

Teachers can step in as mentors to the conductor. They support the conductor by teaching study skills. They ensure the musicians get proper training by paying close attention to individual performances and coordinating any support or tutelage needed for effective performance. A competent symphony orchestra takes years to build through persistent efforts by innumerable dedicated people who believe that music is important. Likewise, academically competent students develop through years of school and the persistent efforts of the adults in their lives who believe they are capable of success and provide them with what they need.

ANNOTATED SELECTED BIBLIOGRAPHY

Anday-Porter, S., Henne, K., & Horan, S. (2000). *Improving student organizational skills through the use of organizational skills in the curriculum.* Unpublished master's thesis, Saint Xavier University and Skylight Professional Development. Retrieved June 8, 2006, from Education Resources Information Center.

Authors note that students with deficiencies in organizational strategies are less likely to be successful in school. Drawing on the solution strategies put forth by other researchers, this group designed an intervention focused on time management, priority setting, study skills, and materials organization. Analysis showed that explicit teaching, practice, and evaluation of the learned organizational strategies increased student organizational skills and improved homework completion and class preparation.

Anderson, D. (2006). *Prof. Darlene Anderson presents on organizational skills instruction.* Retrieved June 13, 2007, from Brigham Young University, McKay School Links Web site: http://education.byu.edu/news/2006_features/anderson_osi.html

At two national conferences, Anderson presented findings that students who were explicitly taught and guided in their practice of organizational skills and goal-setting improved their grades in their core academic classes.

Bakunas, B., & Holley, W. (2001). Teaching organizational skills. *Clearing House*, 74(3), 151–154. Retrieved June 6, 2006, from WilsonWeb.

In response to Kerr and Zigmond (1986), who found that a majority of high-school teachers believe that organizational skills are crucial for school success, the authors map out a list of objectives and related strategies in two categories of organization: supplies and behavior.

Barry, L. M., & Moore, W. E. (2004, March). Students with specific learning disabilities can pass state competency exams: Systematic strategy instruction makes a difference. *Preventing School Failure*, 10–15.

Authors conclude that students are more successful when they are given class time to practice good organization.

Landmark School, Inc.

Bender, D. S. (2001). Effects of study skills programs on the academic behaviors of college students. *Journal of College Reading and Learning, 31*(2), 209–216. Retrieved November 18, 2005, from Education Resources Information Center.

Author concludes that students enrolled in a study skills course and attending required tutoring sessions more often exceed predicted grade point average than control groups.

Benz, C. R., & Fabian, M. P. (1996). Assessing study skills of students with learning disabilities. *Clearing House, 69*(6), 349. Retrieved November 18, 2005, from EBSCOhost MasterFile Premier.

Authors investigate the diagnostic tool LASSI (Learning and Study Strategies Inventory) for use with high-school students with learning disabilities. They conclude that LASSI can help teachers individualize learning and study skills programs.

Blair, C., & Razza, R. P. (2007). Relating effortful control, executive function, and false belief understanding to emerging math and literacy ability in kindergarten. *Child Development, 78*(2), 647–663.

Authors conclude that the executive function of inhibitory control is clearly related to early math and reading ability.

Boyle, J. R., & Weishaar, M. (2001). The effects of strategic notetaking on the recall and comprehension of lecture information for high school students with learning disabilities. *Learning Disabilities Research & Practice, 16*(3) 133–141.

Authors conclude, "Students who were taught strategic notetaking scored significantly higher on measures of immediate free recall, long-term free recall, comprehension, and number of notes recorded than students in the control group who used conventional note taking" (p. 133).

Brown, T. E. (2006). Executive functions and attention deficit hyperactivity disorder: Implications of two conflicting views. *International Journal of Disability, Development and Education, 53*(1), 35–46.

Author discusses two conflicting views of how attention deficit hyperactivity disorder and executive function are related. Article is part of a special issue devoted to attention deficits.

Brown, T. E. (2007). A new approach to attention deficit disorder. *Educational Leadership, 64* (5), 22–27.

Author offers a clear description of the relationship between executive functions and academic competence.

Caine, G., & Caine, R. N. (2006). Meaningful learning and the executive functions of the brain. *New Directions for Adult and Continuing Education, 110,* 53–61.

In the context of constructivist learning, authors discuss the relationship between meaningful learning and executive function. They call for a constructivist, experiential approach to teaching and learning, and offer general guides to action that include scaffolding as an essential element of effective instruction.

Davis, M., & Hult, R. E. (1997). Effects of writing summaries as a generative learning activity during note taking. *Teaching of Psychology(24),* 47–49.

Authors conclude that summary-writing during note-taking enables students to retain lecture information more effectively than students who do not summarize. On a posttest administered 12 days after a lecture, students in the experimental group had significantly higher retention of information.

DuPaul, G. J., & Weyandt, L. L. (2006). School-based interventions for children and adolescents with attention-deficit/hyperactivity disorder: Enhancing academic and behavioral outcomes. *Education and Treatment of Children, 29*(2), 341–358.

Authors point out that organizational and study skills are important treatment targets for middle- and high-school students with attention deficit hyperactivity disorder. They review the extant literature supporting particular interventions on organizational and study skills, including note-taking, long-term projects, and completing written examinations. Among many helpful précis cited are two studies by Gureasko-Moore, DuPaul, and White (2006; unpublished), who document significant increases in the organizational skills of two small samples of students following training in self-monitoring for organizational skills.

Esters, I. G., & Castellanos, E. F. (1998, November 4–6). *Time management behavior as a predictor of role-related stress: Implications for school counselors.* Paper presented at the meeting of the Mid-South Educational Research Association, New Orleans, LA.

Authors note, "As increasing demands are placed on students, and as academic tasks become evermore complex, students' ability to manage time and stress becomes an essential component for academic success" (p. 3). Authors conclude that "perceptions about control of time and preference for organization are statistically and substantively significant predictors of role-related stress" (p. 5).

Fatata-Hall, K. (1997). *Acquisition and application of study skills and test taking strategies with eighth grade learning disabled students failing social studies*. Unpublished practicum report, Nova Southeastern University. Retrieved June 20, 2007, from Education Resources Information Center.

Author concluded students with learning disabilities who were failing social studies improved their grades by participating in classes that taught them good organizational strategies.

Finstein, R. F., Yang, F. Y., & Jones, R. (2007). Build organizational skills in students with learning disabilities. *Intervention in School and Clinic, 42*(3), 174–178.

Authors offer 20 quick suggestions for helping students improve their skills.

Fisk, C., & Hurst, B. (2003). Paraphrasing for comprehension. *The Reading Teacher, 57*(2), 182–185.

Authors review the research on how paraphrasing aids comprehension.

Fountain, R. L. (1992). *Development of a study skills packet to improve grades in ninth and tenth grade students*. An unpublished practicum report, Nova University. Retrieved November 21, 2005, from Education Resources Information Center.

Author finds a strong correlation in grades improvement as a result of a three-pronged intervention: teacher in-services on study skills techniques, including time management, reading textbooks, taking notes, and taking tests; student lessons for those skills; and circle meetings responding to the program.

Gettinger, M., & Seibert, J. K. (2002). Contributions of study skills to academic competence. *School Psychology Review, 31*(3), 350–365. Retrieved December 8, 2005, from EBSCOhost Academic Search Elite.

Asserting that "effective study skills are associated with positive outcomes across multiple academic content areas and for diverse learners" (p. 350), the authors delineate essential components of effective study skills instruction, grouping them into four clusters based on an information processing framework.

Graff, G. (2004). *Clueless in academe: How schooling obscures the life of the mind*. New Haven, CT: Yale University Press.

Author offers practical ways to invite students to participate effectively in intellectual "conversation" about academic subjects.

Gureasko-Moore, S., DuPaul, G. J., & White, G. P. (2006). The effects of self-management in general education classrooms on the organizational skills of adolescents with ADHD. *Behavior Modification*, 30(2), 159–183.

Houston Community College System. (2002). *A study of GUST 0303: Examination of enrollment, demographics and success factors*. Unpublished data, Office of Institutional Research, Houston Community College. Retrieved from Education Resources Information Center.

> Draws conclusions from three years of data collected on students enrolled in a college study skills/orientation course. Course included time management, goal-setting, note-taking, and test preparation. Students who completed the course had significantly higher course completion rates, grade point averages, and return-to-school rates than those who did not complete the course.

Hsieh, P., Sullivan, J. R., & Guerra N. S. (2007). A closer look at college students: Self-efficacy and goal orientation. *Journal of Advanced Academics, 18*(3), 454–476.

> Presents research findings on students' reasons for attrition at the college level. Identifies self-efficacy and goal orientation as the two factors related to underachievement. Authors suggest "teachers should identify those students with not only low self-efficacy, but those also adopting performance-avoidance goals" (p. 455).

Huber, J. A. (2004). A closer look at SQ3R. *Reading Improvement, 41*(2), 108–112.

> Offers a critical review of the small body of research that exists on the SQ3R method.

Hughes, C. A., Ruhl, K. L., Schumaker, J. B., & Deshler, D. D. (2002). Effects of instruction in an assignment completion strategy on the homework performance of students with learning disabilities in general education classes. *Learning Disabilities Research & Practice, 17*(1), 1–18.

> Authors evaluated the effects of instruction on assignment completion rates and quality by students with learning disabilities in general education classrooms. Results indicate that direct strategy instruction in organizational behaviors can increase the rate and quality of homework completion by students with learning disabilities, but that instruction in organizational skills alone is not enough. Student motivation, student skills mastery, and the appropriateness of the given assignments were also important factors.

Kachgal, M. M., Hansen, L. S., & Nutter, K. J. (2001). Academic procrastination prevention intervention: Strategies and recommendations. *Journal of Developmental Education, 25*(1), 14–24.

Authors present results of a study of procrastination among college students and recommend, among other interventions, that students be encouraged to develop self-regulation strategies for time management. These strategies place a heavy emphasis on task analysis and long-term planning, which can help students enhance their performance and achieve their goals.

Kaminski, P. L., Turnock, P. M., Rosen, L. A., & Laster, S. A. (2006). Predictors of academic success among college students with attention disorders. *Journal of College Counseling, 9*(1), 60–71.

Authors conclude that the academic success of students with attention deficity/hyperactivity disorder is positively correlated with time management skills.

Kerr, M. M., & Zigmond, N. (1986). What do high school teachers want? A study of expectations and standards. *Education and Treatment of Children, 9*, 239–49.

Authors found that a majority of high-school teachers believe organizational skills are crucial for school success. In response, Bakunas and Holley (2001) mapped out a list of objectives and related strategies in two categories of organization: supplies and behavior.

Kiewra, K. A. (2002). How classroom teachers can help students learn and teach them how to learn. *Theory into Practice, 41*(2), 71–80. Retrieved December 9, 2005, from EBSCOhost Academic Search Elite.

Kiewra, who teaches a college-level study skills course, aims this article at college professors wishing to increase their students' learning success. He notes that "Good strategy instructors must know two things: (a) which strategies are effective and (b) how to teach them by embedding strategy instruction into content teaching" (p. 1). The proposed teaching/learning strategies are categorized under the pneumonic NORM, which stands for note-taking, organizing, relating, and monitoring.

Kobayashi, K. (2006). Combined effects of note-taking/-reviewing on learning and the enhancement through interventions: A meta-analytic review. *Educational Psychology, 26*(3), 459–477.

This meta-analysis of 33 studies concludes there is an overall positive effect on learning when students take notes and review.

Lee, S. W., & Von Colln, T. (2003). *The effect of instruction in the paraphrasing strategy on reading fluency and comprehension.* Unpublished manuscript, University of Kansas. Retrieved from Education Resources Information Center.

    In a single-subject study, authors find a positive effect on paraphrasing, comprehension, and reading rate following strategy instruction.

Meltzer, L. (2007). *Executive function in education: From theory to practice.* New York: Guilford Press.

    A textbook that presents a framework for understanding executive function and covers a range of approaches to assessment and instruction.

Metcalfe, J., & Kornell, N. (2005). A region of proximal learning model of study time allocation. *Journal of Memory & Language, 52*(4), 463–477.

    Authors' proposed model indicates that allocation of study time is related to the relationships among choice, perseverance, and judgments about learning.

Peverly, S. T., Brobst, K. E., & Morris, K. S. (2002). The contribution of reading comprehension ability and meta-cognitive control to the development of studying in adolescence. *Journal of Research in Reading, 25*(2), 203–216.

    Authors conclude that comprehension and meta-cognitive control of study strategies is positively correlated to information recall. They call for future research to focus on memory and monitoring strategies.

Robbins, S. B., Lauver, K., Le, H., David, D., Langley, R., & Carlstrom, A. (2004). Do psychosocial and study skill factors predict college outcomes? A meta-analysis. *Psychological Bulletin, 130*(2), 261–288.

    This meta-analysis of 109 college students concludes that the best predictors of college grade point average are academic self-efficacy and achievement motivation.

Rosenman, S. (2006). Reconsidering the attention deficit paradigm. *Australasian Psychiatry, 14*(2), 127–132.

    Author discusses the current debate about attention deficit and executive function, and cautions about the need to avoid the risk that executive function will become "a monolithic explanatory paradigm that will solidify thought rather than remain a loose collection of concepts that will encourage flexibility and imagination" (p. 131).

Shanahan, M. J., & Flaherty, B. P. (2001). Dynamic patterns of time use in adolescence. *Child Development, 72*(2), 385–401.

Authors conclude that students highly engaged in multiple domains tended to remain so across grades, but students focused on only one or two domains frequently changed commitments, school plans, grade point average, future orientations, and gender-predicted time-use patterns.

St. Clair-Thompson, H. L., & Gathercole, S. E. (2006). Executive functions and achievements in school: Shifting, updating, inhibition, and working memory. *The Quarterly Journal of Experimental Psychology, 59*(4), 745–759.

Discusses the relationship of executive function to learning and concludes that structuring learning activities to prevent working memory overload enables students with impaired working memory function to learn more effectively.

Stotter, R., Abikoff, H., & Gallagher, R. (2006). Organizational skills training at the NYU Child Study Center. *Education Update Online*. Retrieved January 8, 2007, from http://www.educationupdate.com/archives/2006/Sep/html/spec-organizing.html

Authors point out, "Children who develop a solid foundation of organizational, time management and planning skills are better prepared to face academic and social challenges. However, most schools do not rely on a systematic curriculum to teach these skills" (p. 1). Authors acknowledge that little research has been done to quantify deficits in organization so educators can track children's progress in this area. Authors have developed the Children's Organizational Skills Scale (COSS) and an intervention to address deficits in organization. A pilot study of the intervention done with children with attention deficit/hyperactivity disorder showed significant improvements in organization and behavior both at home and at school. In 2006–2007, the NYU Child Study Center and Duke University, funded by NIMH, is conducting a large trial of the intervention and compare it with other organizational skills training approaches. The results of this study are much needed and will help point the way to refining how organizational skills are taught in schools.

Suh, S., & Suh, J. (2006). Educational engagement and degree attainment among high school dropouts. *Educational Research Quarterly, 29*(3), 11–20.

> Authors note that developing programs that foster organizational skills increases student engagement in school and, therefore, the likelihood that students will stay in school to obtain higher degrees rather than drop out.

Swanson, H. L., Hoskyn, M., & Lee, C. (1999). *Interventions for students with learning disabilities: A meta-analysis of treatment outcomes.* New York: Guilford Press.

> A comprehensive synthesis of 30 years of research on interventions for students with learning disabilities. Of the authors' many conclusions, most significant for classroom teachers is that strategy instruction is effective. Strategy instruction narrows the gap in performance between children with learning disabilities and their peers without learning disabilities.

Titsworth, B., & Kiewra, K. A. (2004). Spoken organizational lecture cues and student notetaking as facilitators of student learning. *Contemporary Educational Psychology, 29*(4), 447–461.

> Authors conclude that spoken organizational lecture cues increased the organization and detail of students notes by more than one-third, and confirmed that both lecture cues and student note-taking raise achievement.

Willingham, D. T. (2002). How we learn. Ask the cognitive scientist: Allocating student study time. "Massed" versus "distributed" practice. *American Educator, 26*(2), 37–39, 47.

> Author offers evidence to support the effectiveness of the "spacing effect." Spacing study time leads to better memory of material.

WORKS CITED

Brown, T. E. (2007). A new approach to attention deficit disorder. *Educational Leadership, 64*(5), 22–27.

Baer, W. (2007). Teaching strategies for students with learning disabilities. *Accommodations — Or just good teaching? Strategies for teaching college students with disabilities.* Hodge, B. M., & Preston-Sabin, J. (Eds.). Westport, CT: Praeger.

Hsieh, P., Sullivan, J. R., & Guerra, N. S. (2007). A closer look at college students: Self-efficacy and goal orientation. *Journal of Advanced Academics, 18*(3), 454–476.

Pearson, P. D., & Gallagher, M. (1983). The instruction of reading comprehension. *Contemporary Educational Psychology, 8*(3), 317–344.

Robinson, F. P. (1970). *Effective study* (4th ed.). New York: HarperCollins.

Sedita, J. (2001). *Study Skills: A Landmark School Teaching Guide* (2nd ed.). Prides Crossing, MA: Landmark School.

Swanson, H. L., Hoskyn, M., & Lee, C. (1999). *Interventions for students with learning disabilities: A meta-analysis of treatment outcomes.* New York: Guilford Press.

Vener, D. (2002). *Study Skills: A Landmark School Student Guide.* Prides Crossing, MA: Landmark School.